THE WAY OF MY CROSS
Masses at Warsaw

by

FATHER JERZY POPIELUSZKO

Translated by

Father Michael J. Wrenn

Director
Archdiocesan Catechetical Institute
New York

Regnery Books
Chicago

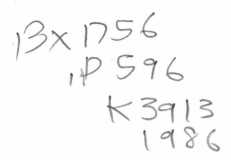

Regnery Books is an imprint of Regnery Gateway, Inc. All inquiries
concerning this book should be directed to Regnery Gateway, Inc.,
950 North Shore Drive, Lake Bluff, IL 60044.

Library of Congress Cataloging-in-Publication Data

Popieluszko, Jerzy, d. 1984.
    The way of my cross.

    Translation of: Le chemin de ma croix.
    1. Catholic Church—Sermons. 2. Sermons, English—Translations
from French. 3. Sermons, French—Translations from Pol-
ish. 4. Sermons, Polish—Translations into French. Lord's Supper—
Catholic Church—Liturgy—Texts. 6. Prayers. 7. Catholic Church—
Liturgy—Texts. 8. Poland—Politics and government—1980-
I. Title.
BX1756.P596C4413   1985   252'.02   85-14469
ISBN 0-89526-806-X (pbk.)

2

CONTENTS

TRANSLATOR'S PREFACE

My first visit to Jerusalem in January 1985 took on a deep and entirely unforeseen dimension. This translation is a direct result of it.

The day after my arrival in the Holy City found me entirely caught up in and deeply moved by the holy places enshrined in the Church of the Holy Sepulchre—the place where Christ was prepared for crucifixion, known to us from accounts of early pilgrims as the *Martyrion*; Golgotha, or Calvary—"the place of the skull," the spot where the cross was lifted high and, a few yards away, the tomb in which the Savior was buried and from which he rose triumphant having conquered death by dying. Morning after morning, sometimes before dawn, saw me making my way from the Damascus Gate, past the *Via Dolorosa* (that "sorrowful way" to Calvary), and down to this sacred place on which the Emperor Constantine had a basilica constructed in the fourth century. Within a few days I had come to know the old city like the palm of my hand and was prizing every new discovery and opportunity for the Scriptures to come alive, even though in most instances my mental image of places and events had to be totally recast in light of the reality staring me in the face.

I was especially fortunate in being the guest of the Dominican Fathers at the distinguished and renowned *'Ecole biblique et archeologique française* in Jerusalem, one of the most important biblical research centers in the Catholic world. Each day upon my return, and usually after dinner, I was debriefed by Father Jerome Murphy-O'Connor, whose best-selling and completely scholarly *Guide to the Holy Land* served as my map of Jerusalem.

One evening after such a session, I visited my host, Father Francis Dreyfus, to wish him a pleasant evening.

As I walked toward his desk I saw, for the first time, *The Way of My Cross*—homilies of Masses at Warsaw—the cover of which bore the smiling but saddened face of Father Jerzy Popieluszko. I borrowed the book from Father Dreyfus and spent the entire night reading it. As I read far into that January morning,I realized that I was doing so in the very area where the first martyr, Saint Stephen, had been put to death. (Actually, the *École biblique* is also known as the Convent of Saint Stephen.) I decided then and there that I had an obligation to translate this absorbing and compelling book of sermons. Rarely had I been as deeply moved as I was by this heroic and courageous priest, who revealed by means of these homilies so much of the depth of his priestly heart. And what tremendous insights into the heart and soul, the profound faith and devotion, of the Polish nation are contained in these concrete applications of the Word of God and traditional patriotic poetry to the plight of a nation, a nation that continues to sustain and cope with centuries of history filled with the cruelest and most demeaning sufferings.

Research at the Polish Institute of Arts and Sciences in New York City and conversations with Professor Samuel Fiszman, of the Department of Slavic Languages and Literatures at Indiana University, revealed to me that Father Popielusko's sermons were based on an old Polish tradition, on the fervent patriotic sermons of Father Piotr Skarga of the 16th century, on Polish folk prayers and supplications, on the political-patriotic-religious writings of Polish Romantic writers, particularly on Adam Mickiewicz's *Books of the Polish Nation and of the Polish Pilgrims*, written in a biblical style and published in Paris in 1832. The comparison between Mickiewicz's *Books* and Father Popieluszko's *Sermons* is especially interesting. The *Books*, imbued with Christian principles written for Polish emigres, were immediately translated into German, English, French and later into many other languages, They also found their way into the patriotic circles of other nations.

Among the numerous books, articles, novels and poems written about the Solidarity years, so full of hope and about the terrible period of martial law, Father Popieluszko's *Sermons* will remain the most faithful testimony to the thoughts and feelings of the Polish people during this time. Polish as they are, these *Sermons* contain universal ideals of freedom for individuals, the most noble religious and patriotic ideals which have an appeal everywhere, and will be understandable and convincing for every human heart striving for nobleness and goodness.

But apart from Father Jerzy Popieluszko's inspiring efforts to lift the spirit of his people, these sermons provide, quite by accident, an inner focus and probe into the day-by-day activity of a regime that was founded and that survives on the Big Lie. Let contemporary Poland, as seen through the eyes of this courageous parish priest, serve as a gauge for measuring the ultimate price paid by other modern communist utopias. These sermons then are meditations on true freedom, man's dignity as a child of God, resignation when faced with suffering and adversity, love and forgiveness without recrimination, and on the fact that there can be no love without justice! They reveal the mind and heart of a great parish priest who, like his Divine Master, laid down his life for his flock.

May our tears be a measure of our own solidarity with him and, above all, with Jesus Christ the model for his priestly existence, and with the Blessed Virgin Mary, Queen of Poland, to him he fled for protection right up until the moment when he died of suffocation, strangulation, and at least thirteen vicious blows unleashed, even more tragically, from the all-too-willing hands of a fellow Pole!

Reverend Michael J. Wrenn
Director
Archdiocesan Catechetical Institute
Saint Joseph's Seminary
Dunwoodie
Yonkers, New York
Feast of the Ascension, 1985

PUBLISHER'S FOREWORD

by Edward R. Kantowicz

Jerzy Popieluszko — an obscure Polish priest with an unpronounceable name — soared comet-like through the Western news media in October, 1984, when he was brutally murdered by agents of Poland's Communist government. His death came as a tragic postscript to a brief but significant chapter in Poland's history, the Solidarity labor movement.

Solidarity began in the summer of 1980, with spontaneous worker protests, followed by a wave of strikes, and culminating in the organization of the first free and independent labor union in the Communist world. Lech Walesa, a charismatic steel worker from Gdansk, led Solidarity on a free-wheeling course for 500 days until the Polish government abruptly outlawed it and declared martial law on December 13, 1981. Fr. Popieluszko had served as chaplain to the workers in Warsaw's steel mills, and had continued to preach the spirit of Solidarity from his parish pulpit after the proclamation of martial law. Government agents abducted, tortured, and murdered him on October 19, 1984.

Fr. Popieluszko's martyrdom — an act with both religious and political significance — reflects Poland's melancholy but dramatic history. The easternmost Catholic country in Europe, located on an open plain with few natural boundaries, Poland has battled for centuries against non-Catholic invaders. The Polish cavalry protected Christian Europe from Turks and Tartars in the Middle Ages. Protestant armies led by the King of Sweden overran the country in the 17th century, only to be defeated by the miraculous intervention of Our Lady of Czestochowa. In 1797 Poland's three neighbors, Prussia, Russia, and Austria, partitioned the country when the name of Poland disappeared from the map of Europe until the First World War.

Three times after partition, in 1830, 1846, and 1863, Poles rose in quixotic, near-suicidal, rebellions against the occupying powers. The country's Romantic poets and writers celebrated the heroes of these rebellions and fashioned an image for Poland as a Christ-like martyr among nations. Just as in Ireland, the Catholic priests in Poland stayed in close contact with their oppressed people and did not permit conflicts to develop between national patriotism and their Catholic religion. As a result, Polish Catholicism fused with Polish nationalism in a deeply messianic longing for Poland's "resurrection." Some even dared to pray, at the end of their litanies, "For a World War, we beseech Thee, O Lord."

The First World War did liberate Poland briefly, but the Second erased its independence once more. The Nazis invaded in September, 1939, overrunning the country within a month. The Russian army, which drove the Nazis out in 1945, installed the Polish United Workers' Party (PZPR) in power; it has ruled Poland ever since, with Soviet backing.

The Catholic Church has served as the only counter-weight to Poland's totalitarian government. Stefan Wyszynski, chaplain to the resistance forces in Warsaw's 1944 uprising against the Nazis, was named archbishop of Warsaw and Primate of Poland in 1948. He negotiated an understanding (porozomienie) with the Communist regime guaranteeing religious autonomy for the Catholic Church in Poland. The Vatican signaled its approval by naming Wyszynski a Cardinal in 1952. Though jailed for his outspokenness in September, 1953, Cardinal Wyszynski was released in 1956 and became a symbol of Polish resistance to the Communist regime. In contrast to other Communist countries, Poland's churches are filled to over-flowing on Sundays and holidays. Church attendance in

Poland carries deeply religious and highly political meaning. Karol Wojtyla, the present Pope John Paul II, and Jerzy Popieluszko, the slain worker priest, were both shaped by this historical fusion of Polish patriotism and Catholic faith.

Jerzy Popieluszko was born on September 23, 1947, on a farm in Eastern Poland near the Soviet border. He left home at the age of 18 to enter the seminary in Warsaw and was ordained a priest in 1972 by Cardinal Wyszynski. Assigned to a parish in Warsaw, Fr. Popieluszko worked with student groups, arranging prayer and bible study sessions and pilgrimages to Czestochowa. Such routine religious activities would not be remarkable in a free country, but in Poland such work was risky. In 1968, the police had shut down student discussion groups at Warsaw University and purged all the universities with massive arrests. Since that time, anyone engaging in organized student activities, even a priest, has been closely watched by the police.

The heroic, but tragic, phase of Fr. Popieluszko's ministry began in the Solidarity Summer of 1980. The striking workers at Warsaw's giant steelworks asked Cardinal Wyszynski for a chaplain, and he assigned Fr. Popieluszko. The priest celebrated Mass for the strikers, within the factory gates, on each of Solidarity's five hundred days. But on December 13, 1981, the Communist regime declared martial law, outlawed Solidarity, and ordered the military to arrest the union's leaders. Special security forces, the dreaded Zomos, tracked down elusive militants and enforced a strict curfew. A grim "Zomo joke" illustrates the macabre, gallows atmosphere of Poland in those days:

> Two Zomos were patrolling the streets of Warsaw five minutes before curfew, when a young man raced by on a bicycle. One of the Zomos raised his rifle and shot the man. His partner

exclaimed, "Why did you shoot him? There's still five minutes until curfew." The first Zomo replied, "I knew where he lived. He'd never make it in time."

No longer able to celebrate Mass at the steel mill, Fr. Popieluszko spoke out from the pulpit of his Warsaw church, St. Stanislaus Kostka. He defended the basic human rights of Solidarity's supporters and demanded justice for those arrested. Parishioners copied down his sermons and distributed them at other parishes and in the universities. Standing-room-only crowds packed his monthly "Masses for the Fatherland," on the last Sunday of each month. Jerzy Popieluszko became Solidarity's prayerful voice during the oppressive months of martial law. The post-Solidarity military regime in Poland, headed by General Wojciech Jaruszelski, harassed Fr. Popieluszko and tried to discredit him. The Central Office for Control of Press, Publications, and Public Performances planted numerous attacks on the priest in the newspapers. The regime opened an official investigation in 1983, charging Popieluszko with "abuse of the priesthood for political ends." Finally, when all this had failed to silence the voice from St. Stanislaus' pulpit, Fr. Popieluszko disappeared.

On October 19, 1984, Jerzy Popieluszko celebrated a late Mass, ate dinner, then left St. Stanislaus in an automobile driven by the parish chauffeur, Waldemar Chrostowski. We only know what happened next because the chauffeur managed to escape and tell the tale of his ordeal that night. A police Fiat followed Fr. Popieluszko's car, overtook it, and forced it to stop. A uniformed police officer ordered the chauffeur out, handcuffed and gagged him, then threw him into the Fiat. Chrostowski heard Fr. Popieluszko struggle and protest, then heard the trunk of the Fiat open and something heavy thud inside. Then the Fiat started up and sped away. Fearing the worst,

Chrostowski risked a jump from the speeding car. A passerby saw him and called an ambulance. Chrostowski convinced the ambulance driver to pick up a priest friend on the way to the hospital. When the ambulance arrived at the hospital, uniformed and plainclothes police were waiting. Were it not for the presence of the priest, Chrostowski too may have disappeared and the fate of Jerzy Popieluszko would never have become known.

The abduction of Fr. Popieluszko could not be kept a secret. When Chrostowski was released and told his story, thousands of concerned parishioners gathered at St. Stanislaus to pray for the safe return of their pastor. Former Solidarity leaders planned protest actions in Warsaw. To avoid violence, Lech Walesa met personally with delegations of outraged workers and persuaded them to stay out of the streets. The abduction was reported on Polish television, and a government spokesman informed the press that a country-wide search for Fr. Popieluszko had been initiated by the police.

On October 25, nearly a week after the abduction, the government announced that a Ministry of Interior "functionary" had been arrested. The next day, the Minister of Interior appeared on television, naming not one but three "functionaries" as the abductors: Grzegorz Piotrowski, Chief of Operations in the ministry's department of worship; Waldemar Chmielewski and Leszek Pekala, both members of the department. The crime had been officially acknowledged and the criminals apprehended, but the body of Jerzy Popieluszko was not found for nearly a week. When the priest's body was finally found, it was discovered that he had been tortured before his death. Grzegorz Piotrowski admitted killing Popieluszko, and all three accused were eventually tried, convicted, and jailed. To draw attention away from themselves, the members of the Communist regime attacked the former Solidarity leaders for exploiting the murder to gain political advantage.

Supporters of Solidarity, in turn, accused the regime of naked terrorism and implicated higher officials in the Ministry of Interior.

Popieluszko's parishioners obtained permission from Cardinal Jozef Glemp, Wyszynski's successor as archbishop of Warsaw, to bury Fr. Popieluszko in a garden near St. Stanislaus. Hundreds of thousands of Poles, including leaders of the outlawed Solidarity, attended the funeral on November 3, 1984. The grave immediately became a shrine for St. Stanislaus' parishioners, Warsaw's steelworkers, and others from all parts of Poland.

Fr. Popieluszko's significance for the Polish people can only be appreciated in the light of Poland's long and troubled history. Jerzy Popieluszko stands in a long line of Polish national heroes who died for "God and country." The opening phrase of the Polish national anthem, written in the 19th century, reads —"Polska jeszcze nie zginela"—"Poland is not dead yet." Jerzy Popieluszko *is* dead, but Poland is not lost. There were heroic Poles in the past, and there will be others in the future.

A fragment of a poem by Czelsaw Milosz, inscribed on a monument to shipyard workers shot to death in 1970, can serve as Fr. Popieluszko's epitaph:

> You who have wronged a simple man, bursting into laughter at the crime. Do not feel safe. The poet remembers. You can slay one, but another is born. The words are written down. . .

Jerzy Popieluszko's words are written down, and now are published in the free world.

TESTIMONY OF FREEDOM

The church in Zoliborz under the invocation of St. Stanislaw Kostka does not differ especially from other churches in Warsaw. Neither in its monumental size, since it was erected in the period between the first and second world wars, nor in strikingness of its modern structure. Nevertheless, it is precisely here that the heart of the city had been beating for these dozen or so months.

In this church masses for the Fatherland were said. The outreach of these masses extended far beyond a single neighborhood. Thousands of Warsaw's inhabitants and religious groups from other cities often came to attend. The church could not accommodate all of them inside and thus they stood in a dense crowd on the square and adjacent streets of Zoliborz, taking part in the services by means of loud speakers. This was *their* hour, which they longed to experience together and with deep concentration at seven o'clock in the evening on the last Sunday of every month.

What do these people crowded together as brothers and sisters feel? What lay behind the common vigor and depth of their experience? An answer to this question can in part be found in this book. It is a compilation of liturgical texts, homilies, and poetry selections which were recited by well-known artists of the Warsaw stage. From these texts we learn that Masses for the Fatherland were and will remain, public reminders of values trampled underfoot, precious values as essential to us as the air we breathe and the food we eat. Truth and freedom are primary among them. I know of no instance where a voice raised in their defense sounded as relevant and to the point as the voice of the curate delivering a homily in the parish church of Zoliborz. It is no wonder that his voice sparked such a powerful response in the hearts of the listeners.

Many of them tried to express their emotions in letters—the authors of which unfortunately must remain anonymous. Frequently mentioned is a motif of hope, which is painfully lacking in everyday Polish life. "The Church gave people hope, so necessary to them now," wrote Agnieszka, who had stated previously that she was a non-believer.

All of this can be discerned in the documents collected in this book. What we cannot experience in any measure is the extraordinary mood which they convey. Sublime and down to earth communality are the first words which come to mind when I recall these services in which I participated. The sense of unity with other people, and at the same time, the awareness that you were part of something went infinitely beyond all of us a sense of being and a real part of our great national tradition.

Although it is difficult to convey these sentiments in words, a few remain indelibly carved in our memory. Here is just one: In February, 1983, I arrived late so there was no chance of my reserving a place to stand on the church square. Together with several close friends, I stood on a street nearby and listened to that familiar voice speaking about the tremendous harm dealt to innocently imprisoned persons, and our responsibility to unite in solidarity with them. A light rain was falling and the assembled crowd was listening carefully. It was then that I suddenly realized that a new chapter in the history of my nation and my city was being written, a history truly worthy of their glorious past.

In the time remaining I would like to say a few words about the people to whom all of us owe a debt of gratitude for this experience. We should all bow our heads to the honorable pastor of the St. Stanislaw Kostka Parish, Monsignor Prelate Teofil Bogucki. We will always be grateful to Father Jerzy Popieluszko, the man who is the soul of this great endeavor. He celebrated almost every mass, compiling the texts, and writing the homilies. In the most cherished sense of the word, he became universally known—human love was focused on him. We recall also the strong affection which the workers of the nearby steel mills felt for their friend and chaplain.

Father Jerzy was a young man whose natural manner and youthful appearance almost made him a peer of the students, whom throughout his priesthood he strove to serve. Inside this modest and sincere person lived a great spirit which spoke through him when he stood at the altar as chaplain. In the words that came quickly to mind there is an answer to the most difficult moral problem of our time: how to combat evil and at the same time avoid hating those who bear it?

Allow me to cite the words with which he ended his homily for August 1982. "Please let us be free from revenge and hatred. We ask for freedom which is the fruit of love. Amen." Together with the Polish chaplain who spoke these words, we say: Amen. So be it.

Klement Szaniawski
Warsaw

THE WORKERS' CHAPLAIN

The tiny room of Father Jerzy's was almost empty. The last guests were leaving. A few hours later they would once again be passing through the factory gates.

I had prepared myself for this discussion for quite some time with their priest, "the Workers' Chaplain"—as he was called by the people of the city. Not a particularly tall man, rather frail, with a boyish face, on which it was hard to discover that illness had been consuming him for years. Rather he gave the impression of a newly ordained priest, and not someone who had spent most of his time in recent years serving individuals who were engaged in hard physical labor.

Q. "Observing you among these workers one gets the impression that you yourself grew up among them?"

A. Actually, I was a stranger to the world of workers. Of course, as a priest performing my duties, I met with all kinds of professional groups. In August 1980 I decided to 'settle down' among the workers. It all began sometime before the last Sunday in August when a delegation of workers from the largest factory in the city came to the bishop with the request that a priest be sent to say the holy Mass on the grounds of the factory itself. The choice fell to me. I shall never forget that day and the Mass as long as I live. I went there feeling terribly apprehensive. After all, the situation was completely new to me. What would I find? How will they receive me? Will there be a place to celebrate the Mass? Who will read the texts and sing? Such questions which now in hindsight sound rather naive, pervaded me as I walked to the factory. It was right there at the gates I experienced my first great shock. Dense rows of people—laughing and crying at the same time—and the applause. I thought somebody important was walking behind me, but it was applause to greet the first priest to cross the gates of the factory since it opened. I remember thinking at the time that it was applause for the Church, which had been knocking persistently at the factory's entrance for over thirty years.

My apprehension was unfounded—everything was ready; an altar stood in the center of the factory's yard, a cross, which later was erected by the entrance, had withstood and weathered difficult times and stands to this day bedecked with bouquets of flowers. A make-shift confessional was set up and lectors were found. You should have heard those deep masculine voices which ordinarily speak frank and employ, putting it mildly, less than unsophisticated words. Here they were reciting the sacred texts with solemnity and deep feeling. Suddenly, like thunder, a thousand workers roar: "Give thanks onto God." I also learned that they could sing quite well, even better than the voices I usually heard in church. Prior to Mass, a number of them had gone to confession. I was seated in a chair with my back practically touching one of the smelters. While these robust peasants dressed in grimy overalls knelt down, the ground turned red from the accumulation of grease and rust."

Q. You do admit, however, that this and similar events were somewhat festive and out of the ordinary, and yet this was in fact, a daily occurrence. It is precisely this festive aspect in which I am interested.

A. To an observer from the outside this could well have appeared festive. Truly, however, it was really quite ordinary. It became an everyday occurrence, or to put it more precisely, it became absolutely necessary. After all, when all is done, it is quite normal for an individual to "discover" and see God outside the walls of a church—in the place where he lives, works, and rests. The Church constantly strove to awaken such an awareness in her believers. For many years we have been teaching people to pray at work and through work, to let Christ be present and a part of one's working place. We recall the Pope's statement: "Open the doors for Christ." Every door—not only to governments and regimes—but also to factories and offices. And so it happened. It was, after all, the workers themselves who had asked us to come and celebrate mass on the premises of the factory. Initially, it may have been spurred on by a sense of danger, a search for support during the difficult moments of the strikes, but as time went on it took on a new dimension: namely that Christ and the Church are assisting them in their everyday work, social activities, and service to others. It was a splendid emotion to feel that Christ and prayer were absolutely essential. I remember their reaction to the news concerning the assassination attempt on the Holy Father. They hung a cloth banner over the altar with the words: "Holy Father, we are praying for you." On that day they wanted to give all they could of themselves. In fact, many of them on that day went to confession for the first time.

Q. But were they able to incorporate Christian values into their daily work and deeds?

A. Perhaps this sounds stereotypical, but what struck me most was the almost daily discovery and growth of their personal dignity, both for themselves and for others. Not that they felt important, nor thought they belonged to an elite class, but they came to realize that every man and woman deserves respect, and they demanded this not only for themselves. What a remarkable change came over them. A second aspect was that they began to take their lives more seriously. They frequently said, "I often went to church, but I did not always understand that this involves making a commitment." Within a few years they began to receive the sacraments. Even those, whose way of thinking up to that time had been quite opposed to religion. And, no it was not all an attempt to ingratiate themselves with their peers. No one demanded this of them, they came to this decision gradually, some after imposition of martial law, during internment, or after the trials. It happened when they realized that the Church was standing along side of them, especially when they felt extremely alone. They saw that the Church, in the name of faith, granted assistance to non-believers, just as they did to all others. And, finally, one other noticeable aspect was their altered attitude towards communal property—their concern and care for the plant, its equipment, and a more honest approach to work.

Naturally, this was not true for all of them. Such changes cannot be brought about overnight.

Q.   What did you personally gain from this work?

A.   I saw how the Gospel can change people. We do not notice this as much, when we as priests meet constantly with believers, usually inside the church, but there I was, and am, a witness to the "awakening" of these people. Never before had I christened so many adults. Do you know what a splendid feeling it is to christen a thirty-year-old man, who prior to this had never heard God? Now not a week goes by without such a christening.

Yes, sometimes I am fatigued. There is simply not enough time for everyone, least of all for myself, but I do not feel weary. It is no longer possible for me to restrict my priesthood to the confines of the Church, even though a numerous number of "counselors" in private told me that a real Polish priest should not go outside the boundaries of his parish. I shall remain among my workers for as long as I am able....

An interview with Father Antoni Poinski

"If I forget you, beloved Fatherland,
let me forget my right hand,
let my tongue dry to my mouth..."

Hence, love for the Fatherland, a warm memory of it in good and bad times—this is indeed the most profound stirring when Holy Mass and prayers are dedicated to its welfare.

Before World War II, every Sunday after High Mass, a prayer was said for the Fatherland and the President of the Republic. This beautiful custom disappeared in the turmoil of war. Years later, the liturgical reforms of the Second Vatican Council eliminated from the worship service all elements that did not pertain to the liturgy, and this prayer was not reinstated. It was possible, however, to incorporate a suitable invocation into the Prayer of the Faithful.

Despite the war's end, the Fatherland continued to flow with tears and blood. It had plunged into the depths of moral turpitude and suffered painful wounds in public life. Favoring the permanent reinstatement of the mass for the Fatherland on the last Sunday of every month, was the result of the bishops' encouragement to pray for the Fatherland, as well as John Paul II's open declarations of love and prayers for the welfare of his native land. The dramatic impact of the pope's visit to his fellow countrymen in June, 1979, inspired an outpouring of love for the Fatherland everywhere.

The first Mass for the Fatherland was celebrated in our church in October, 1980. It was received with great joy. From month to month the number of participants at these prayer meetings increased. After the declaration of martial law, the masses were celebrated by Father Jerzy Popieluszko. The masses for the Fatherland, and those who suffered for it, were attended by crowds of believers. Renowned artists participated by reading texts, and eventually these patriotic masses became widely known throughout Poland and the world.

Father Prelate Theophilus
Pastor of the Parish of St. Stanislaw, Kostka in Zoliborz

1982

I pray you,
to assume all this spiritual heritage which has as its name
Poland, to accept it with faith, hope and love—as Christ
has given it to us through Baptism,
never to doubt it, never to tire of it, never to renounce it,
to have confidence in spite of weakness, to always seek
strength of soul in One in whom so many generations of
our fathers and of our mothers have discovered, never to
abandon Him,
never to lose this freedom of spirit to which He calls
mankind.   (John Paul II, Cracow, June 10, 1979)

FEBRUARY 1982

Entrance Song
We will not abandon your temples, O Christ,
We will not allow the faith to be buried.
Vain are the attempts of evil minds,
Vain are their attacks.
We will defend Your ways.
And God will help us.
From all the temples, houses and fields
a sublime hymn will rise up;
Long live Jesus Christ the King
in the crown of eternal glory.
The trumpet will sound, Long Live Mary.
And God will help us.
Behold, we swear, our hand held high
Sons and daughters of Poland
The Saviour and His Cross will testify
And also the Queen of Jasna Gora.
We will not know rest until the enemy flees.
And God will aid us.   (The Catholic Rota)

Before Holy Mass

In the midst of the storms of this sea of woe,
We do not demand of you, O Mother of God,
to throw down our enemies into woe,
under the yoke, in sickness, an unforeseen death,
slavery.
When our boat encounters the tempest,
We will not petition you, that we might live,
and that they perish crashed upon the rocks.
We will not ask that of you,
but only to separate us from them,
to give us refuge of peace and of tranquility upon
earth,
in which their face will be far distant
in which their voice will be farther still
and that your protection alone remain,
Mother of God, now and for always,
for ages and ages,
so that our heart will not tremble each day
At each moment in pain and uncertainty,
while awaiting cruel and determined invaders,
who hold back law by means of injustice!
                    (Lygmunt Krasinski, "The Prayer," excerpt)

Introduction to the Liturgy

We gather together in the name of Jesus Christ.

We gather together in order to place our prayers on the altar of Christ, but also everything that is being given to us to cope with during this trial of the entire nation.

We particularly include in our prayer those who are the most sorrowfully affected by the state of war. We include in our prayer all those who are deprived of liberty, arrested, interned, dismissed from their work, they and their families.

We also include in our prayer all those who are at the service of the lie and of injustice.

Reading: Wisdom 6:1-9
Listen then kings, and understand;
rulers of remotest lands, take warning;
hear this, you who have thousands under your rule,
who boast of your hordes of subjects.
For power is a gift to you from the Lord,
sovereignty is from the Most High;
he himself will probe your acts and scrutinize your intentions.

If, as administrators of his kingdom, you have not
governed justly
nor observed the law,
nor behaved as God would have you behave,
he will fall on you swiftly and terribly.
Ruthless judgement is reserved for the high and
mighty;
the lowly will be compassionately pardoned,
the mighty will be mightily punished.
For the Lord of All does not cower before a personage,

he does not stand in awe of greatness,
since he himself has made small and great
and provides for all alike;
but strict scrutiny awaits those in power.

Yes, despots, my words are for you,
that you may learn what wisdom is and not
transgress; . . .

Meditation Song: Psalm 58:2-5, 7-8
Gods you may be, but do you give the sentences you
should,
and dispense impartial justice to mankind?
On the contrary, in your hearts you meditate oppression,

with your hands you dole out tyranny on earth.

Right from the womb these wicked men have gone
astray,
these double talkers have been in error since their
birth;
their poison is the poison of the snake,
they are deaf as the adder that blocks its ears
so as not to hear the magician's music
and the clever snake-charmer's spells . . .

God, break their teeth in their mouths,
Yahweh, wrench out the fangs of these savage lions!
May they drain away like water running to waste,
may they wither like trodden grass . . .

Song before the Gospel
Man does not live by bread alone
But from every word which comes forth from the
mouth of God.

Gospel: Matthew 5:13-16
You are the salt of the earth. But if salt becomes taste-
less, what can make it salty again? It is good for nothing,
and can only be thrown out to be trampled underfoot by
men.

You are the light of the world. A city built on a hill-
top cannot be hidden. No one lights a lamp to put it under a tub. They put it on the lamp-stand where it shines
for everyone in the house. In the same way your light must
shine in the sight of men, so that, seeing your good works,
they may give the praise to your Father in heaven.

Declaration of the Bishops and Primate of Poland
The Church always finds itself situated on the side

of truth. The Church is always on the side of people in pain. Today the Church places itself alongside those who are deprived of liberty, of those whose consciences are being broken. The church today puts itself alongside Solidarity on the side of workers who are often relegated to the level of disturbers of the peace.

Last December 15, the Polish bishops declared, in a very special way, the following:

"The superior Council of the Polish Episcopate, gathered together because of the situation of martial law and basing itself on available information concerning the state of the fatherland, addresses to the faithful of the Catholic church some words of encouragement, of unity, and of fraternal compassion.

Our sorrow is that of the entire nation, terrorized by military might. Many active members of the union movement have been interned.

The internments are affecting larger and larger circles of workers, of intellectuals, of students . . . The uncertainty and powerlessness of the world of workers is stimulating an increase of emotion, of bitterness and of hatred even to the point of exasperation . . . The dramatic decision of the authorities to establish a state of war in our country is a blow aimed at the hopes and the expectations of society as these relate to the possibility of resolving the problems of our fatherland by dialogue . . .

We wish that the Church and society concentrate on the following aspirations: (1) The freeing of those interned, and in the interim, their being assured of humane conditions—for we are aware of numerous cases of inhuman treatment, such as that of holding certain of the interned without heavy clothing in places with freezing temperatures.

(2) The restoration of union activities in accordance with their statutes, particularly those of the Solidarity union—this implies the possibility of free activity by its

president[1] and by the union presidium. The union, Solidarity, which defends the rights of workers, is necessary for restoring balance to the life of society.''

And on January 6th, on the Feast of the Epiphany, the primate of Poland stated, ''More and more groups of workers are being requested and ordered to sign declarations that vary in content but are principally aimed at their leaving Solidarity.

This demand is contrary to morality. For some people a conflict of conscience follows: on the one hand the feeling of personal dignity and respect for their own opinions guaranteed by numerous Polish and international legal documents and on the other, the threat of unemployment and condemnation to inactivity as well as the feeling of depriving the country of a qualified worker, for only people of character and, therefore, people of value, have problems of conscience. Conscience is a very special sanctuary. Even God does not violate consciences, but he will judge us according to our consciences.''

Again, on January 19, the Polish bishops declared, ''We particularly address our best wishes to all of those who suffer, therefore to all those who are interned, arrested, condemned, to those who experience sorrowfully the absence of their kin, to those who suffer because of their opinions, to those who are deprived of work. With love and special cordiality we salute the children who are expecting to have their fathers or their mothers back home again. We salute with Christian compassion the families of those who weep . . .''

The vocation of liberty is indissolubly linked to the nature of every man and to a national adult conscience. Also the vocation joins together law and duty, and thus every man and every nation must experience the limitation of liberty as a sorrow and an injustice.

The limitation of the liberty due to man leads to pro-

[1] Lech Walesa

testations, to revolt, and even to war. The vocation of liberty goes along with the equal duty of understanding that liberty is not anarchy, but a duty placed upon every man, demanding reflection, balance, and wisdom in choice and decision.

In considering this truth, that the vocation of liberty is a right of every man and of every nation, we call on all those on whom respect for liberty—particularly each man's freedom of conscience and opinion—depends, to give the greatest priority to this love of liberty felt so vividly by our nation. The consequence of this respect for liberty will have to be the speedy restoration of the normal functioning of the state, the freeing of all those interned, the elimination of tensions for ideological reasons, and the cessation of firings because of opinion and membership in unions.

In the name of liberty, we think that it is important to re-establish, for workers, the right to organize themselves into independent and self-governing unions and for the young, the right to organize themselves into associations that are proper to them.

Universal Prayer
A voice goes up toward You, Lord,
Emerging from the smoke of conflagrations, and from
bloodied clouds of dust
Terrible cry, this final groan
The hairs whiten while listening to this prayer.
(Choral of Kornel Ujejski, 1846)

Before the Blessing
Each final Sunday of the month we pray in our Church asking to have, in our hearts, more love for the fatherland, for its freedom and its independence. Today we pray especially for the intention of those who have been cast aside and put to the test for having loved with

fervor. May they know that all society is with them!

May God give his grace to you who pray for this intention!

May God give his grace to the well-known and admired artists of Warsaw!

Let us thank God for all the good that he does for our country.

Final Song
May God protect Poland
God who has for so many centuries
Enveloped Poland with a brillance of power and of glory,
Who has hidden Her behind His Buckler
In order to protect Her from the wrath which would have beaten her down;
Before Your altars, we bear our supplications
Give us back our Country free, O Lord.

(Alojzy Felinski, 1816)

APRIL 1982[1]

Before Holy Mass
Some crosses and some swords, such is our destiny
And our years succeed one another
And our blood and our pleas
The unwritten pact is sealed
Upon the whole country in this world.

The glory and the sorrow, the bitter harvest
With which you sit before your threshhold
And in vain you seek for a glance from all sides
A wandering old figure bent to the soil
Before your final judge, God.

And our trial which lasts
How to overcome the defeat and the absence of a
pathway
And to bear in one's hand the armor of the cherubim
Lashing out everywhere at evil and distress,
By which we have not yet managed to defeat ourselves.

How, stronger than this the rocks which rain upon us,
Stronger than the free hand and stronger than the
arbitrary and
perjurious hand which beats down upon us,
Cry that we are tireless.
That our heart broken in our breast
Will neither bend nor change.

How rise above the despair and the pains
The heavenly time and the movement of the clock

[1] In March 1982, Father Popieluszko was hospitalized. He was unable to celebrate the "mass for the fatherland."

And read through the centuries the chosen lot
Of their non-written Polish pact;
Death is perishable, faith . . . eternal.
    (K. Wierzynski, Some Crosses and Some Swords)

Introduction to the Liturgy
    The intention of the holy mass that we are celebrating today is the prosperity of our fatherland, peace for our fatherland.

    In the course of holy mass, we will pray especially for those who are deprived of liberty, arrested, interned, condemned, for them and for their families. Even though because of the decision of the authorities, the Solidarity Union may be suspended, may we be permitted this day to mention a special anniversary: exactly one year ago, the bells of our church announced, with a joyous voice, the blessing of the flag of Solidarity belonging to the steel workers of Warsaw. Monsignor Kraszewski represented, on this occasion, our lamented primate.[2] We are therefore going to pray in a special way for the steel workers of Warsaw and for all the steel workers of our country.

Reading: Daniel 3:37-45
Lord, now we are the least of all nations,
now we are despised throughout the world, today,
because of our sins.
We have at this time no leader, no prophet, no prince,
no holocaust, no sacrifice, no oblation, no incense,
no place where we can offer you the first-fruits
and win your favour.
But may the contrite soul, the humbled spirit be as
acceptable to you,
as holocausts of rams and bullocks,
as thousands of fattened lambs:

[2] Cardinal Wyszynski died May 28, 1981.

such let our sacrifice be to you today,
and may it be your will that we follow you
wholeheartedly,
since those who put their trust in you will not be
disappointed.
And now we put our whole heart into following you,
into fearing you and seeking your face once more.
Do no disappoint us;
treat us gently, as you yourself are gentle
and very merciful.
Grant us deliverance worthy of your wonderful deeds,
let your name win glory, Lord.
Confusion seize those who ill-treat your servants:
may they be covered with shame,
deprived of all their power,
and may their strength be broken.
Let them learn that you alone are God and Lord,
glorious over the whole earth.

Meditation Song: Psalm 94:1-8, 20-23
Yahweh, God of revenge,
God of revenge, appear!
Rise, judge of the world,
give the proud their desserts!

Yahweh, how much longer are the wicked,
how much longer are the wicked to triumph?
Are these evil men to remain unsilenced,
boasting and asserting themselves?

Yahweh, they crush your people,
they oppress your hereditary people,
murdering and massacring
widows, orphans and guests.

'Yahweh sees nothing,' they say

'the God of Jacob takes no notice,'
You most stupid of men, you fools,
think this over and learn some sense.

You never consent to that corrupt tribunal
that imposes disorder as law,
that takes the life of the virtuous
and condemns the innocent to death.

No! Yahweh is still my citadel,
my God is a rock where I take shelter;
he will pay them back for all their sins,
he will silence their wickedness,
Yahweh our God will silence them.

Gospel: Mark 13:9-13

Be on your guard: they will hand you over to sanhedrins; you will be beaten in synagogues; and you will stand before governors and kings for my sake, to bear witness before them, since the Good News must first be proclaimed to all the nations.

And when they lead you away to hand you over, do not worry beforehand about what to say; no, say whatever is given to you when the time comes, because it is not you who will be speaking: it will be the Holy Spirit. Brother will betray brother to death, and the father his child; children will rise against their parents and have them put to death. You will be hated by all men on account of my name; but the man who stands firm to the end will be saved.

Homily

God All-Powerful, Lord of our Fathers!

We come before your altar in order to beg you on behalf of liberty in our fatherland.

We humbly bow our head to ask you for the strength

to hang in there and the wisdom to be united. We ask you for your blessing.

We come to you, Lord, on this first anniversary of the consecration of the flag of Solidarity belonging to the steel mills of Warsaw, the consecration of a flag on which is not only written Solidarity, but on which also is found the likeness of your servant, Saint Florian, the watchful protector of steelworkers and firemen. This flag, the pride of thousands of steelworkers who labor so hard, must today be hidden from those who fear the word "solidarity."

One year after the consecration of the white-and-blue flag, the steelworkers, in this place, made a vow that they concluded with these words: "And may God help us!" One of them had composed for this solemn occasion a poem that is also a prayer, a prayer to you, Lord of heaven and earth.

> We, workers, we, ordinary people,
> who bring our flag into your house,
> We pray you, O lord, Bless your faithful people!
> Fill our hearts, Lord God, with burning love.
> The entire country desires, O Lord, your grace
> and your peace,
> Bless us, O Lord God, bless Solidarity!

And you have blessed them, eternal God, you have blessed Solidarity.

For as the primate of the millenium, namely our beloved Cardinal Stefan Wyszynski, said last year, on the second of April: "In the course of these few months, Solidarity has done so much more than the most effective political organization would have been able to achieve." Solidarity has shed light upon evil and its machinations; it has shown to the young generation many of the truths regarding the history of our country that have been suppressed. And we wanted to work so much more for your glory, O Lord and for the wellbeing of mankind. We wanted to work so much more for peace, to construct your kingdom on earth in peace, upon our martyred Polish soil. However, it was to be otherwise.

Today, merciful God, there are so many families of orphans in our Fatherland! Today, so many children await the return of their fathers or their mothers deprived of liberty. Today, parents await the return of their children, husbands await their wives, wives await their husbands.

We pray especially for them that the time of their trial and woe might be ended.

In order that they might be able to cope, give strength of soul to prisoners, arrested and arraigned, because they wanted to remain faithful, to the very end, to the promise which they made before the flags and before the likenesses of the saints, give strength to those who have been placed on the same level as criminals and ne'er-do-wells, offenders of the common good, give strength to the sons of the nation condemned to long trials and prison.

Hear, O Lord, the prayer of your people!

We pray you, Lord, for those who do not know what they are doing, who do not realize that they are adding to human misery by increasing the anxiety and the anguish of their fellow citizens.

Hear, O Lord, the prayer of your people!

We pray, Father, for those who are breaking human consciences. Conscience, the Holy Father has recently said, is what is most sacred, and to break consciences is worse than killing, than physically causing death. You, yourself, O Lord, you do not break consciences. That is why we beseech you that these consciences of our compatriots not be subjugated.

Hear, O Lord, the prayer of your people!

We beg You, almighty Father, for the administrators

of justice who do not have the courage to stand up against the lie but accept what is false for truth.

Hear, O Lord, the prayer of your people!

We beg you for young students in high schools and universities. Grant them, Lord, honesty in thought and action.

Hear, O Lord, the prayer of your people!

As for those who are hiding and who are pursued even today like criminals, grant, Almighty God, that they meet, on the way of their tribulations, some people of kindness and compassion.

Hear, O Lord, the prayer of your people!

We confide to you, O Lord, the workers who have given their blood and who have offered their lives to defend their inalienable human rights. Give them, O Lord, an eternal reward in your Kingdom.

Hear, O Lord, the prayer of your people!

Allow us, O Lord, to address to you a prayer based on the verses of Zymunt Krasinski, our national poet, beseeching you: "that our heart not tremble each day, when at each moment in pain and uncertainty we anticipate the cruel and determined invaders who hold law captive by unjust means."

Hear, O Lord, the prayer of your people! Amen.

Prayer
Our Father, Our God, who art in heaven,
look upon our Country with a charitable eye,
help, by your power, this unfortunate Country,
surround it with a cloud of your grace.
By our humiliation, by the anguish of families
May Your Name be sanctified, may Your Name be
sanctified.
So that this Country may be enriched by the work of men,
that it may be the same Polish house for all,
that the evil overseer not squander its goods,

*that he not destroy the Nation by war and unexpected
disorder.
By our labor, our efforts and our pains,
may Your Kingdom come, may Your Kingdom come.
Strengthen the Church so that it may proclaim Your Will,
so that it may kindle the flame of faith in hearts;
that they find comfort in You for their pains and their
sorrows,
Be a consolation, for us and our brothers.
In You our strength, our hope, our sustenance,
May Your Will be done, may Your Will be done.
Preserve, O Lord, this Country from woe and from hunger,
cause the land of Poland to be able to nourish all of us,
we do not want to be a burden for another nation,
let our own strength raise us up from the fall.
Our modest daily bread today,
allow us to consume it, O Lord, allow us to consume
it, O Lord.
Hold back, O Lord, Your hand which punishes,
Show mercy to Your people.
By Your suffering and Your martydom,
help us on this thorny road to good.
Our faults, by Your agony on the Cross,
deign to pardon them, O Lord, deign to pardon them,
O Lord.
Before the heart becomes hard like a rock,
casting far away the feeling of pity,
give us mastery of ourselves, O Lord.
Do not let us stew in wrath and rage,
pardon our enemies, our oppressors and our traitors,
pardon those who have offended us, pardon those who
have offended us.*

(Anonymous; this *Our Father*
was written by the prisoners of the
camp of Mielecin)

Prayer after Communion

O Land, bereft of sowers and of laborers
Plunged headlong into the miseries of ruins, into the
distress of orphans and of widows!
You have put on again the clothing of mourning, it is
not because of despair.
But in order to harden yourself in a patient and
confident courage!
You rest Your sorrowful head against the flaming door
And you bless with Your sorrow the tribe of Your sons.
You have been deprived of everything, but You are
everything
As long as heaven and earth remain firmly under
Your feet!
O People of Poland! The holiest among the saints will
save you,
She will lift you up from the deep valley of your tears.
Your earth is parched and stricken by the sword
Like the face of the Most Blessed Madonna of Jasna Gora.
(Leopold Staff)

It is a house which appears as a prison
In which our stalwart songs are imprisoned
In which our cry is imprisoned, and no one hears it
In which our eyes cannot see the day through the window
But down below, no day
Only eternal night.
Grills close upon our cries and our glances,
All around, no one, except walls of silence.
And we are there all alone
And we are all there together.
(Anonymous)

You who have wounded the simple man,
Breaking out in laughter before his distress,
Surrounding yourself with a court of fools,

For the confusion of good and of evil,

Even if all bow down before you,
Attributing wisdom and virtue to you,
Striking medals of gold to your glory,
Happy to have survived for a day,

Don't you believe yourself secure. The poet remembers.
You are able to kill him—Another poet will be born,
Deeds and words will be written down.

A winter's dawn would have been much better for you
And the rope and the branch bent under the weight.

[3] (Czeslaw Milosz, 1950, French translation by Anna Turowicz and Constantin Jelenski, in *Poems* 1934–1982, Luneau Ascot Ed., Paris, 1984)

MAY 1982

Before Holy Mass
God, who has made us Polish,
who has nourished us with the Polish soil,
who has allowed Yourself to be glorified and praised
in the Polish language
We beg you, deign to bless our Polish Land!

Bring it about that holy concord and peace reign in
Poland,
together with pious confidence, pious resignation,
liberty and
independence, fraternal love, moral sensitivity, work!
Grant that its people grow each day in virtue!

Hold back, O God, by your sacred power
that which can harm us, and cover us with shame.
Give to us through Your Paternal will what can help
and what can sanctify us.

With the souls of our ancestors already admitted to
heaven,
We lift up toward You this humble plea
in the midst of this disaster, in every sorrowful hour
Have pity, have pity on this Polish Land!
>   (Excerpt from an ancient collection of
>   patriotic and religious poems)

Introduction to the Liturgy
We are gathering together before the altar of Christ in
this month of May. During this month, consecrated to the

Mother of God, a new wave of hatred has just come over our fatherland. In this month, and very particularly in its beginning, a new wave of human suffering has once again broken over us.[1]

By the intercession of the most Blessed Virgin, we want to give, as an offering to God, everything that we have endured in the course of this past month. We wish, through prayer, to join ourselves to the pain of all those who are suffering for justice; we wish to join, by prayer, the sufferings of those who are deprived of liberty, deprived of work—so frequently in the course of this month—deprived of the means of subsistance for their families—there are so very many cases of this.[2] We want to place all of this as an offering to God through the intercession of the most Holy Mother. In today's prayer we beg the very gracious God to transform our sufferings, our pains, and our torments into the indispensable grace necessary for our having a truly Christian attitude in our life. May God bring it about that our trial be transformed by the power of faith and hope to the benefit of ourselves and our fatherland.

Reading: Jeremiah 23:1-5
Doom for the shepherds who allow the flock of my pasture to be destroyed and scattered—it is Yahweh who speaks! This, therefore, is what Yahweh, the God of Israel, says about the shepherds in charge of my people: You have let my flock be scattered and go wandering and have not taken care of them.

[1]   The first and third of May, always considered national feast days by Poles, commemorate the anniversary of the liberal Constitution (May 3, 1791). In 1982 there were violent confrontations in Warsaw and other cities between the partisans, the supporters of Solidarity, and the police. This was the most serious violence since the proclamation of the "state of war."

[2]   Numerous injuries were suffered and deplored, and there were nearly fifteen hundred arrests.

Right, I will take care of you for your misdeeds—it is Yahweh who speaks! But the remnant of my flock I myself will gather from all the countries where I have dispersed them, and will bring them back to their pastures: they shall be fruitful and increase in numbers. I will raise up shepherds to look after them and pasture them; no fear, no terror for them any more; not one shall be lost—it is Yahweh who speaks!

See, the days are coming—it is Yahweh who speaks—

when I will raise a virtuous Branch for David,

who will reign as true king and be wise,

practising honesty and integrity in the land.

Song of Mediation: Psalm 140:2-6, 9-11, 14

Yahweh, rescue me from evil people,

defend me from men of violence,

from people plotting evil,

forever intent on stirring up strife,

who make their tongues as sharp as serpents

with viper's venom on their lips.

Yahweh, guard me from attacks by the wicked,

defend me from those who love force,

from people plotting to make me stumble,

forever laying snares where I walk,

insolent wretches, concealing pitfall and noose

to trap me as I pass.

Gospel: John 19:25-27

Near the cross of Jesus stood his mother and his mother's sister, Mary the wife of Clopas, and Mary of Magdala. Seeing his mother and the disciple he loved standing near her, Jesus said to his mother, "Woman, this is your son." Then he said, "This is your mother" and from that moment the disciple made a place for her in his home.

Before the Homily
Mother of God, Virgin!
Hearken, Mother of God,
To this song of our fathers.
The dawn of liberty appears,
The bell of liberty sounds,
The harvest of liberty increases.

Mother of God!
Bear this song of a free people
Before the divine throne.
Lift your voices, 0 Knights!
That the song of liberty may thunder!
The towers of Moscow will be shaken.
The triumphant song of liberty will break up
The granite icy fastness of the Neva,
Down there also, people possess a soul.

It was the night. . .the eagle with two heads
Was sleeping upon the pinnacle of the edifice,
In his talons he bore steel.
Hearken! The cannons have thundered,
They have thundered. . .and the frightened bird
Flies beneath the crosses of the temples.
He looks—and incapable
Of seeing the nations free
Searches for the shade. . .he leaves for the darkness of
the North.

To arms, brothers! To arms!
Behold the resurrection of the people,
From the somber abyss of humiliation, is at hand,
From the ashes, a new Phoenix,
The people are being lifted up, Bless them, 0 God!
May the song resound like on a wedding day.

Mother of God, Virgin
Hearken! Mother of God,
To this song of our Fathers,
The dawn of liberty is appearing,
The bell of liberty is sounding,
And the blood of freed men is being poured out.

Mother of God!
Bear this blood of a free people
Before the divine throne.

(Juliusz Slowacki Hymn 1830)

Homily

Mother of God! Virgin! Hear us, Holy Mother.

Beneath the cross, you cruelly suffered when Jesus Christ, your Son, was dying. Down there, beneath the cross, Christ has made you our Mother, he has made of us your children. You are therefore our Mother.

King John Casimir chose you for Queen of our fatherland.[3]

You are therefore our Mother and our Queen.

Certainly, you are the best of our mothers; you suffer when you see your children living out their calvary.

Your children are once again prey to suffering during this month of May, which is consecrated to you.

The hatred of those who do not know what they are doing, the hatred of those who do evil and who morally destroy our fatherland—this hatred was especially evident on the occasion of your feast day as Queen of Poland, the third of May.

Many tears have poured forth from the eyes of our

---

[3] In thanksgiving for having helped him to drive out the Swedish invaders, King John Casimir proclaimed the Black Virgin of Czestochowa, Queen of Poland, in 1656.

sisters and brothers. They have received so many blows that they have not deserved.

We implore you, our mother and our queen, on behalf of those who suffer the most; we present to you this litany of our time, of these last six months, of this half year of the slavery of war.

Mother of those who place their hope in Solidarity, pray for us.
Mother of those who are deceived, pray for us.
Mother of those who are betrayed, pray for us.
Mother of those who are arrested in the night, pray for us.
Mother of those who are imprisoned, pray for us.
Mother of those who suffer from the cold, pray for us.
Mother of those who have been frightened, pray for us.
Mother of those miners who were killed, pray for us.
Mother of the workers of the Navy Yards, pray for us.
Mother of those who were subjected to interrogations, pray for us.
Mother of those innocents who have been condemned, pray for us.
Mother of workers, pray for us.
Mother of students, pray for us.
Mother of perservering actors, pray for us.
Mother of those who speak the truth, pray for us.
Mother of those who cannot be corrupted, pray for us.
Mother of those who resist, pray for us.
Mother of orphans, pray for us.
Mother of those who were beaten on the day of your feast, pray for us.
Mother of those who have been molested because they wore your image, pray for us.
Mother of those who are forced to sign declarations

contrary to their consciences, pray for us.
Mother of mothers who weep, pray for us.
Mother of fathers who have been so deeply saddened,
pray for us.
Mother of your servant, Lech [4], cast into prison, pray
for us.
Mother of humiliated scientists and writers, pray for
us.
Mother of suffering Poland, pray for us.
Mother of Poland involved in such a great struggle,
pray for us.
Mother of an independent Poland, pray for us.
Mother of always faithful Poland, pray for us.

We beg you, 0 Mother in whom resides the hope
of millions of people, grant us to live in liberty and in
truth, in fidelity to you and to your Son. Amen.

Prayer after Communion
0 Crowned Queen of Poland, with the scarred face,
To You we lift up our foreheads bent low by the
weight of sorrow.
We do not groan with despair, with parched and
blistered lips,
For a long time we have been praying, wounded we
have prayed
For the grace of faith.
For entire years we march through the night,
soldiers of a tragic cause.
Crosses, crosses behind us, mournful traces of
soldiers.
Remove from us, in the final moment, the sorrowful
bloody cup
The bitterness of the solitary battle.
The poison of treason.

---

[4] Lech is a mythological hero considered an ancestor of the Polish people.
Lech also the first name of Walesa.

In ruins is the church of our childhood, the Cathedral
of Saint John.

At the hour of the final battle, between the walls of
Warsaw in flames,
One sole prayer remains: give us the grace to resist,
0 crowned Queen of Poland,
With the scarred face.

(J. Olechowski, Prayer, 1944)

Nourished with the blood of our brothers, of our dear
Fatherland,
To You this voice is lifted.
Snatch our Country from the infidels
Who are striking it down and tormenting it.
Defend us from the heavy yoke of tyrants
Fight for us with Your weapons
Allow Poland to be without a foreign master,
To take pride once again in your livery.

0 Mother, Mother of the abandoned
The cries reach us without ceasing;
The enemy crushes Your free children
How many widows, orphans among us.
Protect us, protect us with Your Immaculate hand,
0 Most Holy Mother, we beseech You;
You will be as you have been, an effective weapon
Of the Nation which calls you Her Queen.

You have defended us so many times,
Will you do it again this time?
Most Holy Mother, our grave in so short a time is
filled to the very top.

---

* These "litanies of Solidarity" were written in an internment camp
during the state of war.

Tears cover our entire country!
Most Holy Mother, dry them,
Deign to show us your grace,
That the child of Lech not weep.

To you, Our Lady our prayer arises,
We beg your mercy.
See how the enemy buffets our soul,
A deadly fog blinds our eyes.

("Song to the Queen of Poland," excerpt from an ancient collection of patriotic and religious poems)

Before the Blessing

Through the intercession of the most Holy Mother, we pray, faithful people, for the reinforcement of our convictions, for light for our minds and hearts, for the strengthening of our wills.

May we be able to advance each day toward the hope of better days. Let fear and fright be foreign to us when we are certain of our cause. Let us accept the blessing of God for such an attitude regarding life throughout all our days.

JUNE 1982

Before Holy Mass
From our land crushed in misery
A cry goes forth toward heaven,
Do not disdain, 0 Lord, our prayers,
Be receptive to the sound of this song
For, only in You does
the ray of hope shine forth for the poor during these
days of sadness.
0 heart of Jesus, we beg you, save us!
Have pity! Have pity on Poland!

May your heart be moved, 0 Lord,
At the sight of these mournful wounds,
Cease, 0 cease the continuation of this punishment
You who are Father of mercy, 0 Lord!
Do not reject this prayer
by which we beg for Your clemency.

Today, the Nation is in mourning,
Bowed down, 0 Lord, at your feet,
You see, 0 Jesus, the fears, the blood and the chains
And the still fresh tomb of the martyr.
As we are suffering for so long a time,
Break the iron bonds of our slavery. . . .

0 Lord, we do not ask you for vengeance,
We pray to you for our enemies,
Of which we wish to rid ourselves of their yoke,
This yoke which has so greatly wounded our hearts.
0 sweet Jesus, fight in our place with your weapons
Heart of Jesus we beg you, save us!
Have pity! Pity for Poland!

("Prayer to the Heart of Jesus" excerpt from
an ancient collection of
patriotic and religious poems)

Introduction to the Liturgy

We begin the second semester of martial law imposed by the Establishment upon the country. Thousands of persons in our country are deprived of liberty. By the millions, people are suffering. In this month of the Sacred Heart, which has suffered so much, which suffers for justice and peace, we come together in the house of God in order to celebrate the holy sacrifice for the intention of those who are the most affected by martial law: for all condemned, arrested, interned, for those dismissed from their jobs; for them and for their families, and especially for their children.

Reading: Ecclestiastes 9:17-18; 10:1-6, 12
The gentle words of the wise are heard above the shouts of a king of fools.

Better wisdom than warlike weapons, but one mistake undoes a deal of good. Dead flies spoil a bowl of perfumed oil; a little folly is stronger than wisdom and honour.

> The wise man's heart leads him aright,
> the fool's heart leads him astray.

A fool has only to walk along the road and, having no sense, he makes plain to all what a fool he is.

With the anger of the ruler against you, do not leave your post; composure avoids many a fault. There is an evil I observe under the sun, the type of misjudgement to which rulers are prone: folly promoted to high dignities, rich men taking the lowest place.

Words from a wise man's mouth are pleasing, but a fool's lips procure his own ruin.

Meditation Song: Psalm 109:2-9, 30-31
God whom I praise, break your silence,
now that the wicked and the false
> are both accusing me.
They are defaming me,
saying malicious things about me,
> attacking me for no reason.
In return for my friendship, they denounce me,
> though all I had done was pray for them;
they pay me back evil for kindness
> and hatred for friendship.
Give him a venal judge,
find someone to frame the charge;
let him be tried and found guilty,
let his prayer be construed as a crime!
Let his life be cut short,
let someone else take his office; may his children be
orphaned
and his wife widowed!
for conducting the poor man's defense
against those who would have sentenced him to death.

Gospel: Matthew 18:1-7
At this time the disciples came to Jesus and said, 'Who is the greatest in the kingdom of heaven? So he called a little child to him and set the child in front of them. Then he said, 'I tell you solemnly, unless you change and become like little children you will never enter the kingdom of heaven. And so, the one who makes himself as little as a child is the greatest in the kingdom of heaven.

"Anyone who welcomes a little child like this in my name welcomes me. But anyone who is an obstacle to bring down one of these little ones who have faith in me would be better drowned in the depths of the sea with a great millstone round his neck."

Homily

"I beg you, 0 Lord, for this entire land!
Look at it! Hearken to it!
That it does not lose hope in your word.
For God will hear so willingly the voice of a child
When he doesn t ask Him for his own good, but for
that of his brothers."

During this month of June, consecrated to the Sacred Heart of Jesus, we would like to give our heart to those who have the greatest need of it. We would like to accept into our heart the children of families most sorely tried because of martial law—these children who are particularly sensitive to all injustice, which they do not have the wherewithal to understand. The world of a child is a very fragile reality, and the damage caused to the psychological development of the child by evil is even greater when the evil is more violent and cruel; and the encounter with brutal evil and with hatred which has been manifested in so many households from the beginning of the state of war, and since then, can no longer not fail to disturb the mind and heart of children. We have so many orphaned children! children placed in orphanages, lonely and sad children. How much weight on the conscience of these orphaned children as a result of the state of war!

As many of us gather together in common prayer, we address ourselves to you, 0 Lord Jesus, whose heart was pierced by the lance of evil men—you, whose heart has so cruelly suffered.

You have yourself been a child. To you, Son of the Heavenly Father, God has given Saint Joseph, in order to fulfill in your midst his role as earthly father.

You suffered already as a child, when you yourself had, with your parents, to flee-from your fatherland, the henchmen of Herod in hot pursuit.

You understand the sorrow of children whose parents must hide themselves like criminals, which they are not, the sorrow of children whose parents live in camps and prisons.

You understand what the glance that a child directs towards his father signifies, a father preoccupied with the material situation of the family. You understand. That is why, Lord Jesus, we believe we can hear your response:

Dear child, I know your sorrow, for I have suffered with you when evil people armed with decrees for a martial law arrived at night and took away your father. I know that no one will be able to make you forget the days that were passed without him, no more than anyone would be able to make you forget the days that you passed without yourself. But you will learn one day, dear child, that they took him away for a good reason because he wanted to establish justice. And you will be proud of him.

Help us, Lord Jesus, to show us the nobleness of our task in dealing with children orphaned and abused because of martial law. Let no mother escape our concern, our pain, in order to soften her pains.

Give strength, courage, and wisdom to the mothers of children whose fathers are the voice of millions of our compatriots who place their hope in Solidarity. You know, O Lord Jesus, little James of four years to whom his mother, now alone, said with pride: "My son, your father is not here; you are going therefore to replace him." And this son, who asked why "papa" is in prison if he did nothing wrong, sees the eyes of his mother fill up with tears. At the sight of these tears, little James of four years understands in his childlike and moving manner. He understands and he takes care of his mother, in place of his father.

You know the daughter of five years who cries and calls her father on the occasion of a visit to a camp near

Warsaw: "Papa, come home, or let me stay with you here!"

You know, O Jesus, the sufferings and the distress of all the hearts of children and orphans. That is why we believe that the sufferings of children in the entire nation must bear their fruits. What is great and beautiful is born in sorrow. It was the sufferings, the sorrows, the tears and the blood, which in 1970[1] captured the patriotic spirit of youth and which subsequently gave rise to Solidarity. A good tree will bear good fruit. On the tree of evil, the fruits of evil must ripen and rot.

Those who have initiated it say that the state of war is a lesser evil, but it is always an evil. Thus their seeds will bear bad fruit. Bitter will be their harvest.

May this be a declaration, which we are making in prayer; may this be a declaration of sympathy and of solidarity with those who suffer, with those who are molested, deceived, betrayed; may it be our call for the liberation of those who are imprisoned, for the return of jobs to those who have been fired; may this be an appeal that children may know the joy of their young age; may this declaration and this call also be a mighty appeal for the freedom of the fatherland—For a freedom based upon justice, well-being, and love! Amen.

Prayer

You who have offered for mankind the sacrifice of Your blood
To the Father, on the cross and crowned with thorns,
To You, as supplicants, we lift up our hands
For the cup is over-flowing with blood, with bitterness and with tears.
Always crushed, but steadfast in faith,
Our hearts do not tremble at the sight of the wounds,

---

[1] Allusion to the strikes December 1970 on the Baltic that led to many deaths and the fall of Wladyslaw Gomulka.

The armor of our love is forged
We are confident under your fatherly eye.

Your cross, O Lord, we bear it in peace,
Without complaint, groaning, even without doubt,
Wipe from our foreheads the bloody sweat
Comfort us again lest our strength weaken.

Accept, O Lord, accept the innocent blood
Which the enemy has caused to flow from our breasts;
Listen, O Lord, listen to the song of the child
Which sorrowfully reverberates through the city of
Sigismond [2]

And do not submit us, do not submit us to temptation,
Enlighten us with a divine ray of Your Glory
Give eternal salvation to the martyrs,
Stir up fraternal love in the Polish homeland.
Holy, great Lord of miracles
Legitimate Son of the Polish earth
Behold the prayer covered with the blood
Of those who must be free.

Look from heaven at the countryside,
Regard the Polish earth
The voice of sorrow is lifting up,
Save the Polish nation from misery.

Righteousness is breaking down in Poland
A foreign power is crushing us,
It is driving the crown of iron into
Polish temples

Save, save the tormented people.

[2] Sigismond III Wasa, king of Poland who transferred the Capital from Cracow
to Warsaw.

Wake again the valliant Boleslas
Wake again the Jagiellos, the courageous John [3]
May they come forward and confirm our rights.

Wake up again the knights of Raclawice,
And all the defenders of Poland.
May our oppressor be certain that
Liberty does not end.

Saint, holy and just
Hear the groans of your brothers
Behold the children of the Polish homeland
Who seek the assistance of Your hand.

Do not deign, Great Lord,
To allow Polish blood to flow
May it be, O Poland, that God will speak
And Poland will be free.

Wipe the tears of the poor orphans,
Console the wailing mothers,
That the people not die of yearning
At the hand of their executioner.
Obtain for us some years still
In which throughout all the ends of the earth
The people may repeat
Glory and honor to the sons of Lech.

("To Saint Stanislas, Patron of Poland," extract from an ancient collection of patriotic and religious poems)

Do not bury her in a hurry
Do not dig her grave while she is alive
For as long as a single heart beats for her,

---

[3] Celebrated kings of Poland, venerated for their heroism.

She will live in the course of the centuries.
She will lack neither words nor tears
But if your hearts one day are lacking to her
Who will sing for her as mightily
For once your hearts will be silent
She will be dead for all time along with you.

A day will finally come
In which our dream will be fulfilled
In which each instant will be life
And not unceasing death.
Then the Verbum will be renewed
Without useless verbiage.
Each will be able to say
What he sees and what he feels,
What he loves and what he desires.

(Anonymous)

JULY 1982

Letter from the Internees of Bialoleka
Bialoleka July 3, 1982
Reverend Father Jerzy Popieluszko,
We would like to say to you, Father, and to the church of Stanislas Kostka, a very Christian "God will repay you" [1] – and a very warm thank-you for your thoughtfulness, for your assistance through prayer. We warmly thank all those who actively participate in the masses for the internees. We feel ourselves close to you for we are united by the same God, by the same prayer, by the same desires.

We feel ourselves with you when, at the time during which you celebrate holy mass, we are able through our common prayer, to cause to rise from our prison bars the same wishes as those which you express and formulate for our intentions.

Let us help each other. May the spirit of the times and the clashing interests not weaken our resolve. We have to prepare ourselves for renunciations and sacrifices.

A long road lies ahead of us, which we must not abandon, for our own welfare and that of our children. We will hang in there, for you are waiting for us, and the example has been given to us by the martyrdom of Christ, a martyrdom incomparably greater; and we hope that this common suffering will bring to all of us this so greatly desired renewal—the renewal of societal, human, and family life. It will reestablish a European notion of ethics, a Christian system of ethics filled with humanism. We are praying for you.

Hold tight! Hang in there! We will overcome!

---

[1] God will repay you is a popular expression of gratitude.

First Reading: Genesis 4:2-12
The man had intercouse with his wife Eve, and she conceived and gave birth to Cain. 'I have acquired a man with
the help of Yahweh' she said. She gave birth to a second
child, Abel, the brother of Cain. Now Abel became a
shepherd and kept flocks, while Cain tilled the soil. Time
passed and Cain brought some of the produce of the soil
as an offering for Yahweh, while Abel for his part brought
the first-born of his flock and some of their fat as well.
Yahweh looked with favour on Abel and his offering. But
he did not look with favour on Cain and his offering, and
Cain was very angry and downcast. Yahweh asked Cain,
"Why are you angry and downcast? If you are well disposed, ought you not to lift up your head? But if you are
ill disposed, is not sin at the door like a crouching beast
hungering for you, which you must master?; Cain said
to his brother Abel, 'Let us go out'; and while they were
in the open country, Cain set on his brother Abel and killed
him.

Yahweh asked Cain, 'Where is your brother Abel? 'I
do not know' he replied. 'Am I my brother's guardian?'
'What have you done?' Yahweh asked. 'Listen to the
sound of your brother's blood, crying out to me from the
ground. Now be accursed and driven from the ground that
has opened its mouth to receive your brother's blood at
your hands.

Meditation Song: Psalm 27:1-7 12
Yahweh is my light and my salvation,
    whom need I fear?
Yahweh is the fortress of my life,
    of whom should I be afraid?

When evil men advance against me
    to devour my flesh,
they, my opponents, my enemies,

are the ones who stumble and fall.

Though an army pitched camp against me,
    my heart would not fear;
though war were waged against me,
    my trust would still be firm.

One thing I ask of Yahweh,
    one thing I seek:
to live in the house of Yahweh
    all the days of my life,
to enjoy the sweetness of Yahweh
    and to consult him in his Temple.

For he shelters me under his awning
    in times of trouble;
he hides me deep in his tent,
    sets me high on a rock.

And now my head is held high
    over the enemies who surround me,
in his tent I will offer
    exultant sacrifice.

I will sing, I will play for Yahweh!

Yahweh, hear my voice as I cry!
    Pity me! Answer me!

do not abandon me to the will of my foes—
false witnesses have risen against me,
    and breathe out violence.

Second Reading: 1 John 3:13-16
You must not be surprised, brothers, when the world
hates you;

we have passed out of death and into life,
and of this we can be sure
because we love our brothers.
If you refuse to love, you must remain dead;
to hate you brother is to be a murderer,
and murderers, as you know, do not have eternal life
in them.
This has taught us love—
that he gave up his life for us;
and we, too, ought to give up our lives for our
brothers.

Gospel: Matthew 26: 27-38

Then he took a cup, and when he had returned thanks
he gave it to them. 'Drink all of you from this,' he said 'for
this is my blood, the blood of the covenant, which is to
be poured out for many for the forgiveness of sins. From
now on, I tell you, I shall not drink wine until the day I
drink the new wine with you in the kingdom of my
Father.'

After psalms had been sung they left for the Mount
of Olives. Then Jesus said to them, 'You will all lose faith
in me this night, for the scripture says: *I shall strike the
shepherd and the sheep of the flock will be scattered*, but
after my resurrection I shall go before you to Galilee'. At
this, Peter said, 'Though all lose faith in you, I will never
lose faith'. Jesus answered him, 'I tell you solemnly, this
very night, before the cock crows, you will have disowned
me three times'. Peter said to him, 'Even if I have to die
with you, I will never disown you.' And all the disciples
said the same.

Then Jesus came with them to a small estate called
Gethsemane; and he said to his disciples, 'Stay here while
I go over there to pray'. He took Peter and the two sons
of Zebedee with him. And sadness came over him, and
great distress. Then he said to them, 'My soul is sorrowful

to the point of death. Wait here and keep awake with me'. And going on a little further he fell on his face and prayed. 'My Father,' he said 'if it is possible, let this cup pass me by. Nevertheless, let it be as you, not I, would have it.'

Introduction to the Liturgy

I warmly greet all those whom faith in God and the love of the fatherland have brought here. This was our sole intention in inarguarating the solemn holy mass to the glory of God and for the welfare of the fatherland. No other consideration guides us except the one and only good of the fatherland, our mother, much more precious now that she is plunged in pain, sadness, and mourning. We do not wish to castigate anyone but only wish to be allowed to love the fatherland and to pray for her. Whence our joy that this mass for the fatherland evokes such a mighty echo in our society? It is proof that the lot of the fatherland is at the heart of sincere Poles.

It is for us, at the same time an inducement to bring, with even more ardor and fervor, our supplications before the throne of God on behalf of everything that calls to mind the fatherland, for everything that concerns the destiny of Poland. Today we would like especially to recommend to God and to your prayers those who have perished, those who have lost their health for the welfare and the security of the fatherland. Plunged in sadness and sorrow, we present ourselves before the Lord.

Before Holy Mass
Before You, O Lord, who knows what pain is
The thrashing rod, the baseness of slavery,
Crying for Paradise lost,
      Warsaw get up
Before You, who has suffered three days of torment
Who has known the agonies of death
Begging that His pain not be eternal

Warsaw get down on your knees
Before You, dispenser of joy and of grace
You who took pity on your persecutors
The corpse-city, attracting crows by the flocks
  Warsaw bow down
  (W. Gromulicki, "Prayer to the Wonderous Christ in the Cathedral")

Extracts from the Homily of Monsignor Theophilus Bogucki, Pastor of Saint Stanislas Kostka

"And they put Him on the cross."

Christ: insulted, mistreated, agonized on the cross—from his side, pierced by a lance; from his hands and feet, which were dug out; from his temples wounded by the crown of thorns, blood flowed in abundance. It flowed out upon the cross, fell upon the earth, fell upon men. At the price of this blood, Christ redeemed the world. So much Polish blood has irrigated the Polish earth! What is the price of it all?

At the military cemetery of Radzymin near Warsaw, one can see, on the front of the chapel, a fresco representing two angels who are gathering into two golden cups Polish blood spilt on the occasion of the battles of 1920. By the price of this blood, the Polish soldier defended the capitol and the independence of the fatherland. Vilno returned into the arms of its mother country.

An enormous amount of Polish blood irrigated the Polish earth during the last war. . . . For the price of this blood, Poland extended itself to the Oder and the Neisese, as far as the ancestral Szczecin on the shores of the Baltic, although it may always be heartbroken for having lost the beloved Vilno and the heroic Lwow, the gentle Polesia and the rich Volhynie.

Since December 13, blood has flowed once more. But a blood of brothers, the blood of Cain. One brother has risen up against another. Fists were clenched, nightsticks and bludgeons were raised, pistols were fired and blood flowed. What have we gained for the price of this blood? This blood burns us, fills us with shame, with sorrow; it calls upon God like the blood of Abel the just. Those who defended human dignity and the honor of the miner, of the Pole, have fallen. But also have fallen those who do not know what they are doing, drunk with hateful fury, compelled by orders, like the soldiers under the cross.

There were not many who fell, even though no one knows how many; each of them is dear to us, for they are all our brothers, Poles. Today we pray for them, recommending their souls to Divine Mercy. May their blood not have been spilled in vain, may it bring us full and complete liberty, a liberty that is due to us by divine law and not by the pleasure of the prince.

Thus, with our soul in sorrow because of the death of some and the slow agony of others, we beg you, O Lord:

Holy God, Holy Almighty,
Holy Immortal One,
   Have mercy on us!
The Nocturnal terror is settling down on your once
brave people
   Have mercy on us!
We lift ourselves up like ears of corn
Wounded and choked by the weed,
   Have mercy on us!
From foul air, from hunger,
From fire and from slavery,
   Deliver us, O Lord!
From brotherly discord
When drawing water
   Preserve us, O Lord!
From temptation, from sin,
From blaspheming laughter,

Preserve us, O Lord!
We beg you, God,
We sinners,
Hear us, O Lord!
By our fathers in heaven,
Pure and without sin,
Hear us, O Lord!
By the cup filled
With our tears, and with our blood,
Hear us, O Lord!

(Kornel Ujejski, "Supplications," 1846)

Prayer of the Faithful

O all-powerful and merciful God, who has given to the Polish Nation the help and the protection of the Most Blessed Virgin Mary, welcome our prayers which we bring to You today. Permit us to offer them to You through the intercession of Mary, Mother of Grace, Patron of the Capital.

Mother, so many times in the past, have we obtained your assistance. So often that we beg you once again to intercede in behalf of our Fatherland before God, Father of the peoples and of the nations.

We turn toward you, conscious of the time of great difficulty and dangerous changes through which our Fatherland is passing. We come to you with our anxiousness, with our restlessness, yet full of confidence, for you are among us and you envelop us with your motherly protection. You, Mother, You watch over us, You awaken in us the feeling of responsibility for the Fatherland, for the Nation, for its well-being and its destiny. You poured into our human hearts the courage to defend the dignity and the rights of the worker. Today we renew our faith in you. In your hands we place our destiny. Confident, we call on you for help.

Send us light, show us how to triumph over the perils

and chaos of society.

Mother of Mercy, hear us.

Give us unity, a spirit of love, of truth and of understanding, so that we can, above all difficulties and all opinions, safeguard the common good of the Fatherland.

Mother of Mercy, hear us.

Grant us peace of mind, to avoid bloodshed and war.

Mother of Mercy, hear us.

Defend us, so that we do not lose the freedom acquired at the price of so much blood shed by our fathers.

Mother of Mercy, hear us.

Grant us the depth of your grace, a sincere renewal of the soul of the Nation, in order that each of us may undertake the difficult transformation of his personal life by participating in the great work of the social re-birth of the Fatherland.

Mother of Mercy, hear us.

Obtain from your Son, that those who have paid with their lives be welcomed into the Heavenly Kingdom.

Mother of Mercy, hear us.

Mother of God, Mother of Christ, you who stood courageously at the foot of the cross of your Son, come also to our assistance, the assistance of His children. Hear us, and lead us by the way of justice, love, and peace.

AUGUST 1982

Before Holy Mass
Before You, Mother, we kneel
In homage full of gratitude for the grace of
perseverance,
You defend Polish pride before the world,
You defend the faithful people, persecuted by the
tyrant.
 Remain the Star of Wisdom for us
  And may You be Queen of Solidarity
Do not let the calumnious force
Trample ignominiously over our courageous Nation
Be our shield, Mother of Mercy.
 Immaculate Virgin, Mirror of Light,
  Bless Solidarity in Poland.
In the labor of the miner and the peasant,
In the one who does evil to us and makes us sad,
 Be always with us, our Joy,
  Mother of the Poles of Solidarity.
At Your divine call, 0 Mother,
Every man will voluntarily come forth
In order to defend the faith and His Country in need
To be with you everywhere, in heaven as on earth,
 Defend us from all ignominy
  Queen of Solidarity.
Eternal Mother of the Polish Nation,
Remove defeat and hunger from Poland,
 May your protection watch over us
  Pray for us, May you, 0 Mary, be blessed.
  (Anonymous, "Prayer for Solidarity")

Introduction to the Liturgy
 Each month, on the last Sunday, we gather together

before the altar of Christ in order to pray for the liberty of the fatherland, for the liberty that—Monsignor Bogucki said last month—is not given by the good pleasure of the prince, but is a divine right. Man is thus made for freedom, and God himself does not frustrate this freedom. And so all those who restrict human freedom, without having any right to do so, perpetrate a grave evil.

We wish today to include in our prayer whomever is sorrowful in our fatherland, And especially those who are suffering the most for her. In our prayer, we feel ourselves free and in solidarity. Trusting in the aid of the most Holy Mother, Queen of Poland, we cry from the bottom of our heart: carry before the divine throne the prayer of a free people, the sufferings and the tears of a free people!

Reading: Proverbs 2:1-15
My son, if you take my words to heart,
    if you set store by my commandments,
turning your ear to wisdom,
    and applying your heart to truth:
yes, if your plea is for clear perception,
    if you cry out for discernment,
if you look for it as if it were silver,
    and search for it as for buried treasure,
you will then understand what the fear of Yahweh is,
    and discover the knowledge of God,
For Yahweh himself is giver of wisdom,
    from his mouth issue knowledge and discernment.

He keeps his help for honest men,
    he is the shield of those whose ways are honourable;
he stands guard over the paths of justice,
    he keeps watch on the way of his devoted ones.
Then you will understand what virtue is, justice, and fair dealing,
    all paths that lead to happiness.

When wisdom comes into your heart
  and knowledge is a delight to you,
then prudence will be there to watch over you,
  and discernment be your guardian
to keep you from the way that is evil,
  from the man whose speech is deceitful,
from those who leave the paths of honesty
  to walk the roads of darkness:
men who find their joy in doing wrong,
  and their delight in deceitfulness,
whose tracks are twisted,
  and the paths that they tread crooked.

Meditation Song: Psalm 56:2-6, 11-12
Take pity on me, God, as they harry me,
pressing their attacks home all day.
All day my opponents harry me,
hordes coming in to the attack.

Raise me up when I am most afraid,
I put my trust in you;
in God, whose word I praise,
in God I put my trust, fearing nothing;
what can men do to me?

All day long they twist what I say,
all they think of is how to harm me,
they conspire, lurk, spy on my movements,
determined to take my life.

In God whose word I praise,
in Yahweh, whose word I praise,
in God I put my trust, fearing nothing;
what can man do to me?

The Gospel: Luke 6:43-49

There is no sound tree that produces rotten fruit, nor again a rotten tree that produces sound fruit.

For every tree can be told by its own fruit: people do not pick figs from thorns, nor gather grapes from brambles.

A good man draws what is good from the store of goodness in his heart; a bad man draws what is bad from the store of badness. For a man's words flow out of what fills his heart.

Why do you call me, "Lord, Lord" and not do what I say?

"Everyone who comes to me and listens to my words and acts on them—I will show you what he is like. He is like the man who when he built his house dug, and dug deep, and laid the foundations on rock; when the river was in flood it bore down on that house but could not shake it, it was so well built. But the one who listens and does nothing is like the man who built his house on soil, with no foundations: as soon as the river bore down on it, it collapsed; and what a ruin that house became.'

Before the Homily

For the people the source of good and evil resides in the government, and everything that the people experience comes from its hand. Only the government answers before God and before reason for the woes and the misery of the governed. If the blind lead other blind folk, everyone will fall into the same ditch. And what can be said of the blind man who tried to impose, even by violence, his will on the sighted? Why do the saviours of the people tackle a task which goes beyond their capabilities? Who is forcing them to give what they can not attain either by their own means, or by their intelligence, or by their will?

Yes, the people are always correct when they are severe and demanding towards those governing them and when they accuse the governing of the evil that they are forced to endure. Let these stubborn and unwanted leaders of the blind cease their domination over their fellow citizens; let them commit themselves to the way of equality and of the common good, if they do not wish to be treated as the guilty!

The people always refuse their faithful and spontaneous obedience to a government that abandons its position of faithful and devoted servant. They only give in under constraint, and they are absolutely correct. Their first duty is **not** to give in to the domination of a tyrant; otherwise how could their dignity and their freedom as a sovereign people be maintained? What follows are the essential characteristics of every legitimate government:

(1). It must unfailingly continue in its role as servant.

(2). It must give constant proof of its devotion to the people.

(3). It must always owe obedience to truth and to justice.

(4). It must always want to and be able to translate into reality both the ideas and whatever is recognized as correct and just by the most gifted and most virtuous minds.

(5). It must be really capable of creating the common good, not demanding more of anyone than he is able to give and wishes to freely give, and doing this without having to recur either to violence or to any form of constraint toward those being governed.

A government that possesses no other means of intervention than force, is not a government but a usurpation, blasphemy, armed robbery; the people find themselves facing a situation similar to that of a traveler who very calmly is making his way and suddenly encounters an armed, tough, and crafty bandit.

If you have the misfortune of finding yourself face to face with a person of this type, lose every illusion: may you be as innocent and holy as Christ himself, nothing will

be a defense against this person—neither religion nor law
nor any rule or principle. The groans and pleas of Abel
only increased the fratricidal fury of Cain. Recognize then
that you cannot expect anything good on the part of
persons who do not respect your dignity and your
sovereign liberty. . . .

(L. Krolikowski, "The People and the Government,"
in *The Anthology of Christian Social Thought 1831-1864*;
"Ressusciter la Pologne, sauver le monde," Pax, Varsovie,
1981.)

Homily
The Holy Father, John Paul II, in his allocution for the
World Day of Peace, published also by the Polish press,
stated among other things: "Power is a service. To govern
is to serve. The first love of the one governing is love for
those whom he governs. If this indeed were so, if at long
last this great Christian truth were applied to life, if power
were moral, if the principles of administration were
inspired by Christian ethics, how different would ordinary
life, work, and cooperation be. However, we are witnesses
to the actions of tyrannical countries in which citizens
are dealt with as though they were being prosecuted."

In his turn, our own "primate of the millennium,"
Cardinal Stefan Wysynski, who died a year ago, stated on
the sixth of January last year, in reference to the allocution
of the Holy Father: "The citizen has become the worst
enemy of the regime." Why is this so, the primate asked?
And he responded: "Because the citizen has been
deprived of his rights and dissuaded from fulfilling his
obligations. The regime should not be tyrannical," our
lamented primate cried out, "and the state must not be
an organized prison."

Two years ago, during the last two weeks of August,
in sorrow and troubled mind and spirit, in fatigue, both
physical and spiritual, kneeling before improvised altars,

assisted by intellectuals and artists, and carried along by the patriotic spirit of the workers, **Solidarity** was born.

Let us revive in our memories that date: August 31, 1980, when the people gathered together before the gates of the steelworks in Warsaw to participate in the celebration of mass with the striking steelworkers. It was Sunday. Then, in our struggle, we appealed to God for the restoration of the worker's dignity. We know quite well that victory of a just cause cannot be obtained without God.

What can we say today, on this second anniversary of that patriotic initiative—and it is not the first initative of this type!—by Polish society? What can we say, today, when the agreements of Gdansk and of Silesia were broken one night in December last year in such a sorrowful and violent fashion? A blow has been struck, a wound opened, a wound that still bleeds but not a mortal wound, for it is impossible to give a deadly blow to an idea that is incapable of dying. It is impossible to kill hope, **Solidarity** was and continues to be the hope of millions of Poles, a hope so much stronger because it is close to God through prayer.

Solidarity developed in the nation as a powerful tree that, although crushed, continues to have new roots. Some storms have violently shaken the tree, its glorious crown has been torn, but it continues to cling to its native soil and continues to draw into our hearts and our prayers the life-giving juices that allow it to survive in order to one day bear good fruit. .

Despite the sorrowful experience of these last months, the nation is ever ready to work with devotion for the good of its fatherland. But only a nation respected by those governing it, a nation that will not live in uncertainty, constant confusion, and bewilderment, only a nation that does not feel itself being imprisoned will be able, with a glad heart, to undertake this mission. It is not possible to speak of the mutual building of the house when human rights are disregarded, when human dignity is not respected, as was the case most recently, for example, in the internment camp of Kwidzyn, where so many of our compatriots are still being held in camps and prisons.

For this reason, the primate of Poland, addressing himself to hundreds of thousands of pilgrims gathered together at the feet of the Queen of Poland at Jasna Gora, clearly and explicitly determined the conditions necessary for the beginning of the mutual building of our house. It is useless to discuss these conditions, for they are the will of the nation filled with love for the fatherland.

First: the liberation of Lech Walesa. (Applause.)

Second: the freeing of all the interned.

Third: the restoration of unions, the setting up of a process with a view to amnesty, and, finally, the fixing of a date for the upcoming visit of the Holy Father. (Applause).

All this is included in our prayerful intentions during the course of this holy mass that is being celebrated for the fatherland.

We will conclude this reflection with the words of the Holy Father, who prayed for our fatherland as follows:

"Accept this heavy prayer of suffering, you who are Queen of Poland and you, holy patrons of my fatherland. For a long time you have been Queen of Poland! Take under your protection the entire nation, that it may prosper for your glory."

Amen.

Prayer After Communion

The Polish Nation lifts itself up from slavery and from submission, with the manly resolve never again to put on the shackles which it has just broken, nor to lay down the ancestral arms until such time as it recovers its independence and power, the only guarantee of liberty, and until such time that it is guaranteed the liberties to

which it has a twofold right: that of the glorious heritage
of its ancestors and that of the necessary expectations of
this century. . .
(Manifesto of the Diet, January 2, 1831)

There are other countries
In which liberty and the Fatherland
are joined together under the same banner.
In which there is bread and work,
and flowers in the streets.
In which the confidence of a child
is a joy and a right,
and old age as natural
as a prayer of thanksgiving.
Yet the house of my birth,
newly trampled over,
newly wounded,
with fresh crosses upon the graves,
with prison bars.
In which the word is a lie
And silence the law.
In which the day begins
With dread of the dawn
And ends with the uneasiness of the night.
And in which millions of hearts
unite together in prayer
so as not to lack hope
(Teresa, "There Are Other Countries")

Whatever will be, whatever will happen,
that fear and terror totally cover the land,
that the world trembles from one pole to the other,
if holy wisdom is built on peace,
so that this poor land can catch its breath
so that it may unite and bring everything into
harmony.

Even though it happens, even though it comes about,
I know one thing: justice will exist,
I know one thing: Poland will be reborn,
I know one thing: in a matter of centuries
our grave will be changed into a house radiant with
life.
I know one thing: we will cry out with all our heart:
"May You be blessed, 0 Holy Lord, for all ages!"
(Zygmunt Krasinski, "Whatever Will Be, Whatever
Will Happen")

0, brother worker, with hammer and with apron!
Your shops and dark mines are volcanoes.
The stifling yoke of work and the ignominious gold
weigh heavily upon your thoughts and upon your
spirit.
But your soul was eavesdropping, listening for the
sun,
and it will carry the contagious light
into the subterranean pits, and it will untie your
shackled hands.
Those who watched over your chains have grown
pale!
They grasp your hand and declare this a
fraternal handshake. Note well! It is only their
final fitful movement which is attempting to hold back
your hand
armed with the hammer!
(Leopold Staff, "The Rightful Furor")

Before the Blessing

This Sunday we read in the churches the communique of the Polish Episcopate. We would like to emphasize some sentences in this communique:

"The bishops are conscious that the forthcoming second anniversary of the agreements of August 1980 is not only an historical event; it will have very strong repercussions upon the attitudes of Poles and upon the current situation of Poland. For this reason, anxious for the good of the entire nation, we are asking everyone to celebrate this anniversary in a spirit of seriousness and national calm, heightened by common prayer before the altars of the Lord. We are calling all the faithful to prayer.''

Let us receive the blessing for the time of hope.

SEPTEMBER 1982

Introduction to the Liturgy

In the course of this holy Mass for the fatherland and for those who suffer for justice in the fatherland, we will hold crosses in our hands. By this gesture, we wish to emphasize that everything has its meaning in the cross. Everything that is sorrow, suffering, physical or moral pain, everything that we call the cross in each of our lives, the cross of our nation. All of this fully acquires its meaning in union with the cross of Christ.

There is no church without the cross, neither is there sacrifice nor sanctification nor service without the cross. There is no perserverance nor victory without the cross. The person who conquers in a just cause conquers by the cross and in the cross. The church must speak the truth. The Church must defend those who are suffering. In the name of truth, the Church cannot throw an indifferent glance toward evil, human miseries, and pain.

Thus, in its warm and gracious prayer, the Church reaches out in welcome to all the sorrowful concerns of the fatherland. She reaches out in welcome especially to those who are arrested, unjustly condemned, interned, those whose dignity is offended, those who are deprived of their jobs, for their sufferings are in a very special way similar to the sufferings of Christ.

Today is also the first anniversary of the consecration of the flag of the Solidarity union belonging to the workers of FSO. On the side opposite the word *Solidarity*, the image of St. Christopher, patron of drivers, is found. Let us therefore pray for the workers of FSO—may they remain faithful to the commitment that they made the previous year, before the flag bearing the image of the saint.

Reading: Isaiah 50, 4-11
The Lord Yahweh has given me
a disciple's tongue.
So that I may know how to reply to the wearied
he provides me with speech.
Each morning he wakes me to hear,
to listen like a disciple.
The Lord Yahweh has opened my ear.

For my part, I made no resistance,
neither did I turn away.
I offered my back to those who struck me,
my cheeks to those who tore at my beard;
I did not cover my face
against insult and spittle.

The Lord Yahweh comes to my help,
so that I am untouched by the insults.
So, too, I set my face like flint;
I know I shall not be shamed.

My vindicator is here at hand. Does anyone start
proceedings against me?
Then let us go to court together.
Who thinks he has a case against me?
Let him approach me.

The Lord Yahweh is coming to my help,
who dare condemn me?
They shall all go to pieces like a garment
devoured by moths.

Meditation Song: Psalm 86, 1. 3-5. 14-17
Listen to me, Yahweh, and answer me,
poor and needy as I am;

You are my God, take pity on me, Lord,
I invoke you all day long;
give your servant reason to rejoice,
for to you, Lord, I lift my soul.

Lord, you are good and forgiving,
most loving to all who invoke you;
Now arrogant men, God, are attacking me,
a brutal gang hounding me to death;
people to whom you mean nothing.

Lord God, you who are always merciful and tender-
hearted,
slow to anger, always loving, always loyal,
turn to me and pity me.

Give me your strength, your saving help,
me your servant, this son of a pious mother,
give me one proof of your goodness.

Yahweh, make my opponents ashamed,
show them that you are my help and consolation.

Gospel: Matthew 27, 27-31

The governor's soldiers took Jesus with them into the Praetorium and collected the whole cohort round him. Then they stripped him and made him wear a scarlet cloak, and having twisted some thorns into a crown they put this on his head and placed a reed in his right hand. To make fun of him they knelt to him saying, 'Hail, king of the Jews!' And they spat on him and took the reed and struck him on the head with it. And when they had finished making fun of him, they took off the cloak and dressed him in his own clothes and led him away to crucify him.

Homily

Christ died on the cross for all of humanity. He conquered death and he showed the way to resurrection.

Why did the salvation of humanity have to be accomplished on so cruel an instrument as the cross was, in ancient times, considered to be?

It was the Phoenicians who invented death on a cross for the most despised members of the population, for people deprived of every right, such as slaves. If Christ had died by stoning, perhaps he would have been no more than a Jew being put to death. If He had been beheaded with a sword, he would have died as a Roman. But by dying as a slave on the cross, He became the brother of all humanity, for death as a slave touches people of all nationalities. A slave can be a Jew, a Greek, or a Goth. A slave can be illiterate or a man of culture.

Because of the death and resurrection of Christ, the symbol of shame and humiliation became a symbol of courage, of persistence, of assistance, and of fraternity. In the sign of the cross we seize today upon the fact that there is a great deal of beauty and courage in man. It is by means of the cross that we advance toward the resurrection. There is no other way. And this is why the cross of our fatherland, our personal crosses, those of our families, must lead to victory, to resurrection, if we join them to Christ who has overcome the cross.

We can join our sufferings, our crosses, to Christ, for the trial against Christ still continues. His trial always continues because of his brethren. The actors in the drama and in the proceedings against Christ are always alive. Only their names and faces have changed, just as their dates and places of birth have changed. Procedures change, but the trial itself continues. Sharing in this trial are all those who shower sufferings and sorrows upon their brethen and those who struggle against the very thing for which Christ died on the cross. Participating in this trial are all those who attempt to build on falsehood, the lie, and the half-truth; those who humiliate human dignity, the dignity of the children of God; and likewise those who repress, for their compatriots, this gift so precious in the eyes of God himself—the precious gift of freedom, which is either fully eliminated or partially limited. What a resemblnce there is, today, between Christ covered with blood on the cross and our sorrowful fatherland! The poet exclaims,

Christ is stretched on the Cross
like Poland in the time of slavery.
Christ extended on the Cross
like Poland . . .

Like Christ on the cross, the fatherland is covered with his spilled blood. His sons are deprived of honor, of dignity, of virtue; they are humiliated, often they are ill-treated.

His own countrymen killed Christ on the cross, in his own country.

Today, also, our brothers fall by the hands of our own fellow countrymen. We could cite numerous examples to demonstrate that the nation is bearing its cross.

The greatest cross is the lack of respect for the fundamental rights of the human person. Other crosses flow from this. Our late lamented primate, Cardinal Wyszynski, put it this way: "Respect for the fundamental rights of the human person is the first priority of every social order and is the condition for peace in the world, for peaceful consciences, for peace in families, for peace in nations." Wherever human rights to truth, to liberty, to justice, are not respected, peace no longer exists or will not be able to exist. It is, first of all, absolutely necessary to guarantee citizens their fundamental basic rights before attempting to bring together those elements essential to constructing the peace. In our fatherland, these laws are not respected: some thousands of Poles are in prisons and in camps. The media have spread an abundance of lies, and justice is undergoing serious strain and distortions.

The cross of the fatherland is still here: for some decades, a totally counterproductive stubborness has persisted in seeking to remove God from the people, especially from the young, and to impose on them an ideology that has nothing in common with the one thousand-year Christian tradition of our nation. I will quote the words of our beloved primate:

"How can one believe that Poland, which has lived for ten centuries enlightened by the cross and the gospel, could deny Christ and abandon its Christian culture, formed throughout the centuries and deeply imbedded in the private, family, and national life?" This plan to spread atheism, this struggle against God and everything divine is, at the same time, a struggle against the nobility, the greatness, and the dignity of the human being; a man is great because he bears in himself the dignity of the children of God.

The cross is lack of truth. Truth contains in itself the capacity to resist and to blossom forth with the light of day, even if some attempt, with great determination and care, to hide it. The lie always dies a quick death. Truth is always concise and to the point, while the lie surrounds itself with cheap talk and gossip. The roots of every crisis are to be found in a lie.

The cross is lack of liberty. Whenever liberty does not exist, there is no love and there is no friendship between members of the family or between partners in a national community or between nations. By employing force, one is unable to love another or to be his friend. The man of today is more sensible to the action of love than to that of force. It is through the heart that Poles are one, not through threats. And even daring does not consist in bearing arms—our lamented primate recalled—for daring does not depend on the steel of arms but is rooted in the heart.

Each of us who is here could cite a great number of

crosses that have been experienced or witnessed, particularly during the last ten months—months of constant disturbance, of torment, of anguish, months of uncertainty
about tomorrow.

All these crosses of our private and social life must
lead to the resurrection of the fatherland, fully free and
just. Since Christ died on the cross, no suffering, no humiliation, is capable of shaming us. Shame is the lot of
those who cause these crosses.

And just as Christ didn't do an "about-face" on his
way of the Cross, but advanced toward his victorious end,
so our nation, strengthened by Christ, will not turn back,
even if it has to go forward on its aching knees to the resurrection.

We pray God to give us hope, for only strong men,
through hope, will come to triumph over all difficulties.
We pray to be given interior joy, for it is the most awesome
weapon against Satan, who by nature is sad. We pray Him
to deliver us from vengeance and from hatred and to give
us this freedom that is the fruit of love.

Amen.

Prayer of the Faithful
Let us pray . . .
—for the Church of Christ: that it always show forth the
way of truth, of love, and of justice;
—for the Holy Father, John Paul II: that God bless him and
permit him to come soon to his fatherland;
—for the fatherland: that God ordain that it progress happily in justice and freedom;
—for those governing us: that they understand that to
govern truly means to serve in a spirit of love and
fraternity;
—for people deprived of liberty, arrested, condemned, interned, deprived of work and for their families: that they
encounter the assistance and kindness of others;

—for the interned members of the independent union
Solidarity with Lech Walesa at their head: that they, as
quickly as possible, regain their freedom and that they be
once again given the opportunity to work effectively for
the common good of the fatherland;
—for our nation: that it never lose the hope that makes cop-
ing with all trials and difficulties possible;
—for those who have lost life or health during the state
of war: that their sacrifice serve the moral rebirth of our
fatherland;
—for us, assembled here: that we do not lose faith in the
meaning of our sufferings and trials.
Hear us, O Lord.

Prayer after Communion
*Always with humility, from that one so truly hu-
miliated,*
a daily song rises toward You:
God, O God, above poor Poland
Your justified wrath is suspended!
You are just, Lord, O Lord,
You see and know our sufferings.
May this common appeal
reach You, O You, Our Saviour.
Yes, Our Saviour, Poland ensnared
in painful thorns, in its powerlessness,
surrounded by enemies, by words, by blasphemy,
it is the Cross of Golgotha, of Your martyrdom.
Today a spark of living force
surrounded by sorrows is kindled in it.
Polish hearts this day are reunited.
In You help and hope burn brightly.

Now, looking for consolation from You,
this day we knock at Your door with our prayers.
This day we pray the Father of heaven,

in Your Name, by Your merit!
Pardon our offenses, O benevolent Judge.
Establish once again the freedom of our Fatherland,
but this time forever.
Take up, O take up the cause of Polish people.

Lift up the humiliated and strike down the proud and
boastful.
Preserve us from giving in to savage fury,
be always with us and yourself singlemindedly engage
in combat.
Do not punish our persecutors,
they do not know what they are doing.
Always with humility, from that one so truly humiliated,
our daily song rises toward You.
Have pity, have pity on poor Poland!
In blessing transform Your wrath!

("Song to the Saviour of the World," extract from an
ancient collection of religious and patriotic poems)

There is only one Poland, just as there is only one
God in heaven.
All my strength I pledge to it.
My whole life, which comes from You,
I belong entirely to you, my Fatherland.

I venerate the perfect example of your great men,
the holy remains of your heroes,
I believe in Your future filled with great glory,
with power, with well-being and justice.

I know it: not the oppression and self-seeking ag-
gressions
but the freedom of peoples advances under Your

standard.
No past more beautiful than Your own,
no glory greater than to be Polish.

Here I am as a soldier ready for everything,
in the Fatherland and abroad
I wait and I cherish the Polish treasure,
the language, the customs, the Polish spirit.

Bound for always to the Polish Nation,
I sense within myself each moment what She senses,
called to a great common future,
I swear fraternity with all Poles.

                        (Jan Lechon, "Hymn of Polish Émigrés")

OCTOBER 1982

Introduction to the Liturgy

We are living out the eleventh month of martial law in our fatherland. The month of October ends today; once again it has been heavy with sorrowful and tragic events.

Once again the blood of our brothers has flowed this month. The life of the young steel worker has been taken.[1]

In the course of this month the Solidarity union has lost the right to any legal activity. Faced with this fact, the Holy Father stated that this is a violation of the fundamental rights of society and of man; and he gives the assurance that the Holy See and the church in Poland will continue to defend the just rights of workers. In the course of this month, there have been a number of new, large-scale arrests and internments.

This month, consecrated to our Lady of the Rosary, has also known a happy event. One of the sons of our fatherland has been admitted to the honors of the altar and to the list of holy martyrs. We have a patron for suffering Poland.[2]

In offering to God this very holy sacrifice, we are also offering to him everything that we have just experienced; and we wish to pray that he give to us, to us and to our nation, strength of spirit and love of the truth—so that, in spite of external slavery, we can remain free men in mind and heart.

---

[1] On October 8 the Polish Parliament adopted the text of a resolution creating new unions in Poland; this definitively placed Solidarity outside the law. On October 12 the militarization of the Lenin Shipyards at Gdansk provoked a great deal of tension. On October 13 disturbances in Cracow and Silesia led to the death of a young worker in Nowa Huta.

[2] The reference is to Saint Maximilian Kolbe, who died in the concentration camp at Auschwitz during World War II.

Reading: Wisdom 10:8–16
For, by neglecting the path of Wisdom,
not only were they kept from knowledge of the good,
they actually left the world a memorial of their folly,
so that their crimes might not escape notice.

But Wisdom delivered her servants from their ordeals.
The virtuous man, fleeing from the anger of his
brother,
was led by her along straight paths.
She showed him the kingdom of God
and taught him the knowledge of holy things.
She brought him success in his toil
and gave him full return for all his efforts;
she stood by him against grasping and oppressive men
and she made him rich.

She guarded him closely from his enemies
and saved him from the traps they set for him.
In an arduous struggle she awarded him the prize,
to teach him that piety is stronger than all.

She did not forsake the virtuous man when he was
sold,
but kept him free from sin;
she went down to the dungeon with him;
she would not abandon him in his chains,
but procured for him the sceptre of a kingdom
and authority over his despotic masters,
thus exposing as liars those who had traduced him,
and giving him honour everlasting.

A holy people and a blameless race,
this she delivered from a nation of oppressors.

Meditation Song: Psalm 52
Why make a boast of your wickedness,
    you champion in villainy,
all day plotting destruction?
Your tongue is razor-sharp,
    you artist in perfidy!

You prefer evil to good,
    lying to honest speech;
you love the destructive word,
    perfidious tongue!

That is why God will crush you,
    snatch you away for good,
    tear you out of your tent,
uproot you from the land of the living.

Dread will seize the virtuous at the sight,
    they will laugh at his fate:
'So much for the man who refused
    to make God his fortress,
but relied on his own great wealth
    and drew his strength from crime!'

I, for my part, like an olive tree
    growing in the house of God,
put my trust in God's love
    for ever and ever.

I mean to thank you constantly
    for doing what you did,
and put my hope in your name, that is so full of
kindness,
    in the presence of those who love you.

Gospel: John 8:26–32
      'About you I have much to say
      and much to condemn;
      but the one who sent me is truthful,
      and what I have learnt from him
I declare to the world.'

      They failed to understand that he was talking to
them about the Father. So Jesus said:
      'When you have lifted up the Son of Man,
      then you will know that I am He
      and that I do nothing of myself:
      what the Father has taught me
      is what I preach;
      he who sent me is with me,
      and has not left me to myself,
for I always do what pleases him.'

      As he was saying this, many came to believe in
him.

      To the Jews who believed in him Jesus said:
      'If you make my word your home
      you will indeed be my disciples, you will
      learn the truth
and the truth will make you free.'

Homily
      We place ourselves today before the altar of Christ
in front of which is your likeness, O Saint Maximilian,
patron of suffering Poland. We stand before you there in
order to bring our prayer before the throne of God, to dialogue with God, through you as intermediary, in our name
and in the name of all those who suffer in camps and in
prisons, in the name of those who suffer because they
fought for justice and truth in the fatherland. All the high

emotions of recent years, those that are linked to the election of a Pole to the Holy See, those that are linked to the first visit of the successor of Peter to Polish soil—the entire first visit recapitulating the course of the Polish nation's rich history—and also those that come from the birth of Solidarity, all this has strengthened us and has prepared us to cope valiantly with the sufferings and the humiliations that we have had to endure for more than ten months.

But the fact that you are counted among the saints, you, Father Maximilian, martyr of our own time, this fact shows us and confirms us in the conviction that the power of evil, of the lie, of spite, and of hate must be surmounted. You are, Saint Maximilian, the symbol of the victory that man, subjugated by force, yet remaining free in his soul, carries deep within himself.

Remaining free in the soul necessarily means living in truth. To live in truth is to give witness to the truth. It is to lay claim to it and recognize it in every situation. Truth is unchangeable. We cannot destroy truth by decisions or by decrees. Slavery for us consists rightly in this: that each day we submit ourselves to the reign of the lie. We do not protest; we silence ourselves, or, actually, we make it seem as though this can be believed. Then, we live in the lie. The courageous testimony of truth is a way that leads directly to freedom. The man who witnesses to truth is a free man even in external conditions of slavery, even in a camp, in a prison.

If, in the present situation, the majority of Poles entered into the way of truth, if this majority did not forget what was true for it for at least a year, we would, from then on, become a nation free in soul, and the external or political freedom would come sooner or later as a consequence of this freedom of soul, of this fidelity to the truth.

The essential problem for the liberation of man and the nation is to overcome fear, for fear is born of threat. We have a fear of suffering, a fear of losing a possession, of losing freedom, health, or a position. We act then against conscience, which is an index of truth. We overcome fear when we accept suffering or the loss of something in the name of higher values. If truth becomes for us a value for which we are willing to suffer, to take risks, then we will overcome fear, which is the direct cause of our slavery. On more than one occasion Christ told his disciples: "Do not fear. Do not fear those who kill the body, they cannot do anything more." You, Saint Maximilian, you remained faithful to this teaching of Christ. You had no fear about leaving for the unknown territory of Japan in order to speak the truth about Christ. You weren't afraid to suffer or lose your life. Because of that, your free spirit lives and bears fruit.

Our lamented primate of Poland, Cardinal Stefan Wyszynski, imprisoned for having spoken the truth, wrote in his notes of October 5, 1954: "Fear is the greatest shortcoming of apostles. . . . It frightens the heart and constricts the throat. The one who is silent before the enemies of a just cause makes them bolder and more determined to reduce to silence by means of fear; such is the first objective in this impious strategy. . . . Silence has its own proper apostolic meaning only when I do not turn my face from those who strike it." This is what the primate said in his notes from prison.

We truly have need of you, Saint Maximilian, as a model of the man who does not give in to fear, who does not let himself be frightened. We need a saint whom we can invoke as the patron of suffering Poland. For which of the saints would be able to pray more fittingly than you for his nation that is today enslaved? You, who have been beaten and ill-treated, and have seen your brothers frightened along with you, in prison and then in the camp and in the starvation bunker. You were locked up without trial merely because you were a son loving the fatherland and the truth. You accepted suffering and death in place of someone else.

To accept suffering willingly in place of someone else is more than to suffer. Only one who is interiorly free can make such a decision.

Today there are among us some people who are exercising the power of sympathy in society: some simple workers also have declared themselves ready to go into an internment camp in place of mothers and fathers of families. They wished to bear the cross of their brothers, they wished to free some families of suffering, wherever necessary. Unfortunately, they have not been given the opportunity to make this sacrifice for their brothers.

Our nation has suffered much in the course of centuries. It is very difficult for us, even today, to speak of the sorrowful past, of the terrible years of the occupation; but the more we remember what our nation underwent in the past, under the hatred of the occupier, the more we understand the words of the Holy Father addressed to Poles during the audience of last October 11:

"It is not good," the Holy Father, profoundly moved, said, "It is not good that Poles come to assist at the canonization of their compatriot with tears in their eyes, for these are not tears of joy. . . . Sometimes there were appeals, some appeals not only in this hall but appeals from far away; and that is why I wish to respond to these appeals through you who are here. I wish to respond to those who are absent and particularly to those who are in internment camps, in prisons. I would like to respond to all those who suffer in the land of Poland, and I want to address myself here to the authorities of the Peoples' Republic of Poland, so that these tears cease. The Polish society, my nation, does not deserve to be pushed to the point of shedding tears of despair and of dejection, but it deserves to have a better future created for it."

Yes, a nation that has suffered so greatly in its recent past does not deserve to have many among thousands of its sons and daughters dwelling in camps and prisons; it does not deserve to have its youth beaten and mistreated or that the crime of Cain be committed. It does not deserve being deprived, against its will, of the Solidarity union, which has paid its dues through the suffering and blood of the workers; this union, which the lamented primate of Poland, as early as April 2, 1981, said had done more than the best political organs could have done in a few months; this union, which the Superior Council of the Epicopate said last December 15, is indispensable for reestablishing a proper balance in social life; this union, whose restoration has been called for consistently by the present primate of Poland; and this demand is based on his own authority and that of the entire Church.

We have a vocation to truth. We are called to witness our life of truth. "You will know the truth," Christ exclaimed in the passage of the gospel that we have just read," and the truth will make you free." Let us then be faithful to the truth.

We conclude this reflection with the words of a prayer that we beg you, O Saint Maximilian, to bring to the throne of the Lord by the intercession of our very holy and Immaculate Virgin Mother, whom you have served throughout your life.

We end this reflection by recalling the words pronounced by the Holy Father when he was still Archbishop of Cracow: "Weak are a people if they accept their own defeat, if they forget that they have been sent to watch until their hour comes; for the hours ceaselessly return on the huge sundial of history." May the hour of truth come quickly upon the huge clock, the heroic clock of our nation! May truth finally triumph in our fatherland! Amen.

Prayer of the Faithful

Let us pray . . .

—for our martyred fatherland, that through the prayer

of Saint Maximilian, God will preserve it under his protection and watch over it and preserve it from all danger;

—for the Holy Father, John Paul II, cruelly tried by the problems of our fatherland, that God give him strength of soul and that he be permitted to meet Poles on their own native soil;

—for those governing us, that they remember that to govern really means to serve with humility and love;

—for those who are deprived of liberty, arrested, condemned, interned with their leader, Lech Walesa, that they soon recover freedom and that they take up again the tasks that society has conferred upon them;

—for the militant members of Solidarity who must hide, that, in their tribulations, they find some compassionate and well-disposed people;

—for those who have been fired from their jobs, particularly this month, that God grant them special blessings;

—for those who have lost their lives or health during martial law, that their suffering and their sacrifice hasten the advent of a truly free and just Poland;

—for those who are at the service of the lie and of injustice, that God open their hearts and help them to see the reality of their humiliating activity;

—for the soldiers of the Polish army, that in remembering the noble traditions of the Polish armed forces, they never soil uniform or honor by lifting their hands against their nation;

—for all of us gathered here in prayer, that we never lose hope in the final triumph of good, which is being prepared for through suffering.

We pray you, O Lord, hear us.

Prayer after Communion
You were like a big old tree,
my people, hardened like the oak,

animated by lively vigor,
a tree of faith, of strength, of furor.

Some butchers set about gnashing you,
quartering your roots,
in order to change your appeal and your form,
in order to transform you into a scarecrow.

They have set about tearing and cutting your leaves,
so that you may be naked and so that you may bend
your head in shame.

They have set about burning your eyes,
so that your look cannot transform them into corpses,
They have set about transforming your body into
ashes,
in order to snatch God from your living soul.

And behold you hold yourself erect, alone, naked,
like a deadly specter behind the bars,
half suffering, half destroyed,
ploughed under by fire, by the yoke, by tears.
But the heavenly clock turns
and time strikes the buckler with its sword,
and you bathe yourself in the clear light of heaven
listen to your heart: your heart is beating.

And you arise, like God from His grave.
The earth will open its arms before you
in a gasp of a tornado-like whisper.
My people! To arms!
      (Krzysztof Kamil Baczynski, "You Were Like a Big
                          Old Tree," April 1943)

Mary, Mother of the Polish soil
And our hope in everything

This confidence makes us live today
In this evil hour protect us.

It is you, Mother whom we love
From the Baltic to the Tatras.
This confidence makes us live today
In this evil hour protect us.

May the darkness become light
May the hour of truth come.
This confidence in you makes us live today
In this evil hour protect us.
You who defend us
Do not abandon us, Mother, today.
Confidence in you makes us live today
In this evil hour protect us.

("Mary, Mother of the Polish Homeland,"
sung during the strikes
in August 1980 at the Baltic.)

NOVEMBER 1982

Before Holy Mass
We stand humbly before You
We lift high the crosses of our suffering.
Pray for us, O Mother, come intercede with God
In order that He may give to all the grace that we need, the
grace of forgiveness.

To those who have been lifted up
Unaware of the fact that only power, given by the people is holy,
And who, creating new laws forget
That the memory of those who dispense evil will be cursed.
Give us the grace to pardon their flunkies
Who, clasping in their hands the silver pieces of Judas,
as recompense for their shameful acts,
They will ever remain foreigners among their own.

And when each day the despair and the sorrow cut across
The villages and the cities of this tormented land
Give us, O Mother, the grace, the grace of forgiveness,
Before the cup of bitterness should overflow.
(Teresa, "Prayer of Forgiveness")

Reading: James 5:1–8
Now an answer for the rich. Start crying, weep for the miseries that are coming to you. Your wealth is all rotting, your clothes are all eaten up by moths. All your gold and your silver are corroding away, and the same corrosion

will be your own sentence, and eat into your body. It was a burning fire that you stored up as your treasure for the last days. Labourers mowed your fields, and you cheated them—listen to the wages that you kept back, calling out; realize that the cries of the reapers have reached the ears of the Lord of hosts. On earth you have had a life of comfort and luxury; in the time of slaughter you went on eating to your heart's content. It was you who condemned the innocent and killed them; they offered you no resistance.

Now be patient, brothers, until the Lord's coming. Think of a farmer: how patiently he waits for the precious fruit of the ground until it has had the autumn rains and the spring rains! You too have to be patient; do not lose heart, because the Lord's coming will be soon.

Meditation Song: Psalm 57:2–8, 10–11
Take pity on me, God, take pity on me,
in you my soul takes shelter;

I take shelter in the shadow of your wings
until the destroying storm is over.

I call on God the Most High,
on God who has done everything for me:
to send from heaven and save me,
to check the people harrying me,
may God send his faithfulness and love.

I lie surrounded by lions
greedy for human prey,
their teeth are spears and arrows,
their tongue a sharp sword.

Rise high above the heavens, God,
let your glory be over the earth!

They laid a net where I was walking
   when I was bowed with care;
they dug a pitfall for me
   but fell into it themselves!

My heart is ready, God,
   my heart is ready;
I mean to sing and play for you,
   awake, my muse,
awake, lyre and harp,
   I mean to wake the Dawn!

Lord, I mean to thank you among the peoples,
   to play music to you among the nations;
your love is high as heaven,
   your faithfulness as the clouds.
Rise high above the heavens, God,
   let your glory be over the earth!

Gospel: Luke:21, 25–28, 34–36

There will be signs in the sun and moon and stars;
on earth nations in agony, bewildered by the clamour of
the ocean and its waves; men dying of fear as they await
what menaces the world, for the powers of heaven will
be shaken. And then they will see the Son of Man coming in a cloud with power and great glory. When these
things begin to take place, stand erect, hold your heads
high, because your liberation is near at hand.

Watch yourselves, or your hearts will be coarsened
with debauchery and drunkenness and the cares of life,
and that day will be sprung on you suddenly, like a trap.
For it will come down on every living man on the face of
the earth. Stay awake, praying at all times for the strength
to survive all that is going to happen, and to stand with
confidence before the Son of Man.

Excerpts from the Homily of Msgr. Theophilus Bogucki

We recall today the sad time of a century and a half ago. Three cruel occupiers had dismembered the living organism of the nation and were gleefully rubbing their hands for having blotted out Poland from the map of Europe.

Justifiably, one night in November 1830, young candidates at the Infantry School of Warsaw took up arms and showed to the world that Poland was alive, that hope was not dead. The entire capital marched behind them. The uprising spread throughout the entire country. . . . The revolution was repressed with great bloodshed. And, in punishment, there was constructed at Zoliborz that dismal edifice of the citadel in which the defenders of liberty were tortured and condemned to death.

All the revolutionary and liberation movements were, none the less, a sign of the life of the nation and a proof of its right to freedom. The one who put a stop to the life and liberty of the nation committed a crime just as a person commits a crime who puts an end to life that has just been conceived, or who assassinates a human being.

Poles died in dungeons, in prisons, in Siberia, but they never lost hope of recovering a free and independent fatherland. Commandant Valerian Lukasinski, hero of the November uprising, chained and condemned to perpetual solitary confinement in a fortress, did not cave in. A pathetic, old, sick and deaf man, he survived in prison until the uprising in January 1863. When the insurgents were imprisoned, he asked them only one question: "Is Poland alive?", for he always bore Poland in his heart; he suffered for her and, even though he agonized over her, he did not lose the hope that she would live. During all the years of hard slavery, of the cruel occupation, the nation, trusting in God and in his most Holy Mother, never lost heart. The enemy himself stated that the Polish nation, for which no hope shown forth, still reverenced the church and the

Black Madonna of Jasna Gora.

Experiencing several centuries of bitter sufferings has taught us where to look for help, to whom to go with confidence. The greater the nation's suffering, the greater will be the triumph. This Sunday opens the holy season of Advent, a time of expectation, a time of hope. Let that hope be present in our hearts. Let us mutually console one another, give comfort to one another, and help one another to live through these difficult days.

There are already some glimmers of hope that this trying period, of martial law, will end and that all men unjustly condemned, those in hiding and those on the run, will return to their homes and that a period of love, unity, and liberty will finally come at last.

Between your hands, Mother and Queen, our sole hope, we place our destiny and the lot of the fatherland.

Amen.

Prayer of the Faithful

Let us pray for . . .

—the Holy Father, John Paul II, that he may be able to visit his fatherland and strengthen the hope and resolve of Poles;

—for our martyred fatherland, that its progress take place in true liberty and justice;

—for those governing us, that they allow themselves to be inspired by the spirit of service and of justice for the common good of the fatherland;

—for those who are deprived of liberty, arrested, condemned, dismissed from work, ill-treated, those submitted to questioning, for those who have been forcibly expelled from the fatherland, that God and men of good will have a special concern for them;

—for the members of Solidarity who are interned and condemned, that they recover their freedom in order to work effectively on behalf of the common good of the fatherland;

—for Lech Walesa, that he keep alive the ideals for which, as the head of the workers, he has struggled;

—for those who during the state of war have lost their lives or their health, that their suffering and their sacrifice serve the moral renewal of our nation;

—for those who are at the service of lies and of injustice, that they rediscover human dignity in themsleves;

—for the militia, that they remember that they are sons of this nation and that they not lift their hands against their brothers;

—for us, gathered together here in prayer, that we never lose the hope that allows us to surmount the worst trials;

Hear us, O Lord!

Prayer After Communion
Holy God!
We are fighting for a just cause;
For our liberty
for our land and our sea;
for the Cross that the mother traces upon the
forehead,...
for Polish bones in the Wawel,
for the cemeteries of our fathers,
in which Your sign shines,
for the years passed and the years to come,
for our mountains and the Vistula,
for our women and our children,
for our destiny close at hand and our destiny far off,
for the rights of God and those of man.
For everything. . . .
Hear our call,
You who are with us,
Lord, all powerful,

Give us victory!
>   (Casimir Wierzynski, "Holy God," fragments, War-
>   saw, August 30, 1939)

from the blood of brothers which is being spilled forth,
from the price which the appeal of the workers
is going to have to pay,
>   Preserve us, O Lord!
from tribulation and fright,
from the knowledge that we are being strangled,
from fear of the future,
>   Preserve us, O Lord!
From the deprivation of our children,
from the enslavement of minds,
from pains and from vengeance,
>   Preserve us, O Lord!
From tortures inflicted on the young
from the humiliation of our humanity,
from those who lie,
>   Preserve us, O Lord!
From the rupture of the human chain,
from ignominy of soul,
from foolishness,
>   Preserve us, O Lord!
From the profanation of all which is sacred and holy,
from doubt regarding whether or not there is some-
thing greater,
from the evils of separation,
>   Preserve us, O Lord!
For national solidarity,
for everything which is new,
for a pure life,
>   Give us strength, O Jesus!
>   (Anonymous; internment camp of Goldapia)

DECEMBER 1982

Before Holy Mass

Today we wish to pray together:

That Solidarity and all unions recover the rights of which they have been deprived;

That the Lord bless all our actions undertaken for the common good and the glory of the Fatherland.

Our thoughts and our sentiments are directed this festive evening toward the Holy Father in Rome. We wish to share our heart with him, as we share in this host. We wish to express to him our cordial gratitude for his efforts to make Poland known throughout the world, and for his continual prayers for the intentions of the Fatherland, addressed to Our Lady of Jasna Gora.

God preserve and give him long years of life. We assure you, beloved Holy Father, that in these times of despair, we are not losing hope. And, lifting high the crosses, we sing the hymn of victory: Christ, Lord, O you who are Christ, you govern us.

Introduction to the Liturgy

We gather together before the altar of Christ and we pray for the Fatherland and for those who suffer the most on her behalf.

During the month of December the sorrow and joy, suffering and hope, are in a special way mingled together.

Sorrow: so vivid and close to our memory are the anniversaries of the deaths of our worker brothers killed in 1970 and 1981.

Suffering: since many brothers and sisters remain behind prison bars.

Hope: that the regime, despite everything, will work for the true good of the fatherland and that we will feel ourselves to be the masters of our own destinies. Even when betrayed, hope never dies.

Joy: for behold, it is God who is coming toward man. He makes himself the poor infant in the crib of Bethlehem in order to strengthen people of good will in the struggle for the common good, for freedom, for justice.

In this common prayer, we offer all these pains and these joys before the altar of Christ and we ask him to change them into graces of hope for the triumph of good over evil.

We have a particularly moving sentiment from those who yesterday were interned and today arrested. They address to us the following best wishes from the camp of Bialoleka:

"In this day of the nativity of the Lord, we are especially close to and in solidarity with the entire human community. Despite the separation, our hearts and our thoughts are present among you and we participate in this holy mass and in this common prayer which ascends to God in behalf of the happiness of all in our fatherland. Against our wills, our bodies remain separated from you; but we are with you in spirit, the spirit of Solidarity, and in the desire for serving the common good and combating evil. May God help us."

Reading: Galatians 5:1, 7–10, 13–15

When Christ freed us, he meant us to remain free. Stand firm, therefore, and do not submit again to the yoke of slavery.

You began your race well: who made you less anxious to obey the truth? You were not prompted by him who called you! The yeast seems to be spreading through the whole batch of you.

My brothers, you were called, as you know, to liberty; but be careful, or this liberty will provide an opening for self-indulgence. Serve one another, rather, in works of love, since the whole of the Law is summarized in a single command. *Love your neighbour as yourself.* If you go snapping at each other and tearing each other to pieces, you had better watch or you will destroy the whole community.

Meditation Song: Psalm 64:2–6, 8–9
God, hear me as I make my plea,
protect me from this frightening enemy,
hide me from the wicked and their schemes,
from this mob of evil men,

sharpening their tongues like swords,
shooting bitter words like arrows,
shooting them at the innocent from cover,
shooting suddenly, without warning.

Urging each other on to their wicked
purpose,
they discuss where to hide their snares.
'Who is going to see us?' they say.

God will shoot them with his own arrow,
wound them without warning.
He will destroy them for that tongue of theirs,
and all who see them fall will shake their
heads.

Then all will feel afraid,
will tell others what God has done;
they will understand why he has done it.

Gospel: John 10:11–16
I am the good shepherd:
the good shepherd is one who lays down his
life for his sheep.
The hired man, since he is not the shepherd
and the sheep do not belong to him, abandons the sheep and runs away
as soon as he sees a wolf coming,
and then the wolf attacks and scatters the
sheep;
this is because he is only a hired man
and has no concern for the sheep.
I am the good shepherd;
I know my own and my own know me,
just as the Father knows me
and I know the Father;
and I lay down my life for my sheep.
And there are other sheep I have
that are not of this fold,
and these I have to lead as well.
They too will listen to my voice,
and there will be only one flock,
and one shepherd.

Homily

"Fatherland, there is nothing there of affected pathos, but the great heritage of difficult centuries of Polish history."

In order to recall the year that has shot by,
we are going to use today the words of the Holy
Father, words of his prayer, the prayer that, on
different occasions, he addressed to the Virgin
for the intention of the Polish people.

In the words of this prayer, which he repeated throughout the year of martial law, he recapit-
ulates the thoughts that express his deep and
abiding concern for our country. In these words

he sets forth all his own personal sorrow and suffering. He, who is the finest son of our nation, was and is always the one who confirms in us the hope that evil, constraint, hatred, and humiliation of human dignity may finally be set aside. He stimulates us to struggle in solidarity for the defense of basic human rights.

In January of this year he called upon our Lady of Jasna Gora in this prayer:

"Why, for your sixth centenary celebration, have they prepared, for you and for all of us, this situation, this state of war, in a country that has every right to the fatherland of a sovereign nation?"

Responding to the letters of the interned and those who, on the occasion of the nativity of our Lord, had written to him, he stated, "Be with us, and we are with you"—he prayed thus:

"Be with us, with us—imprisoned, condemned without trial to loss of freedom, with us all who are suffering because our neighbors are imprisoned. O Mother, help us; you yourself, you have been imprisoned! Your image of Jasna Gora has been imprisoned on the occasion of its journey through Poland. But it recovered liberty. Mother, I beg you, that all those who are unjustly deprived recover their freedom."

In February, on his return from Africa, he addressed himself to Poles in these words: "I will never forget the great plaza of Kaduna in Nigeria, where I ordained priests from among black deacons: in the midst of hundreds of thousands of persons there was found a group of Poles; above them floated a white and red flag with the inscription *Soldiarity*." Then the pope explained that Solidarity is not only a name for suffering but is, first of all, what we experience in thinking of those who are being interned each day in the fatherland because of their work for the rights of man and the sovereignty of the nation. "Solidarity is not only the name of this punishment and pain. It is also the name of unity and of community. ... Solidarity has a profound and demanding content of which Poles in the 1980s have taken hold. This sorrowful and difficult content is passing through a sorrowful purification."

Unfortunately, this sorrowful purification was brutally interrupted.

In a prayer last March the pope took up again the words of the Polish bishops in stressing what constitutes the components of society: ". . . the governing power and the legitimate representatives of organized social groups, among which there can never be excluded the representatives of those unions temporarily suspended—primarily those of the independent union Solidarity, which enjoys such widespread social acceptance."

We know today that it will be very difficult to build this social peace and harmony because a union that enjoys the support of millions of people has been suppressed by martial law, and it is very difficult for us to believe once again in a social compact since those in whom the workers had confidence were arrested a few days ago. We will believe only when the act of abolishing this state of war guarantees freedom to those who have been interned.

In place of internment, our brothers were being given the choice of leaving their native country until, from the city of the successor of Peter, these clear and strong words fell like a ton of bricks: "Today, at the moment in which our nation is undergoing a new trial, we cry out to you, Mother of Jasna Gora: there is no place in Poland that is not for Poles. Each man has the right to his fatherland. No one can be condemned to exile."

On the occasion of the anniversary of the attempt on his life, the Holy Father, through tears of sorrow, said:

"Since December 13, I have once again been suffering with my nation. Why cannot its character as a moral person, to which it has a right, be restored? Why continue with the alienation of the state by building the state on repression? Why deprive that state of its sole strength, its character as a moral person that belongs to the nation? Accept my prayer, heavy-laden with suffering, you who are Queen of Poland! . . . The nation cannot develop correctly when it is deprived of these rights that condition its full character as a moral person. And the state cannot be strong by sheer dint of every type of repression."

One well might add: do not struggle by means of repression. Repression is not a proof of force but of weakness. One who is incapable of winning over by the heart or by reason tries to win by repression. But each manifestation of repression is a proof of moral inferiority. The most magnificent and longest remembered battles that history recalls are the battles of human thought. The most reprehensible and the most easily forgotten are the battles of repression. The idea that needs arms to perdure dies of itself. The idea that can only be maintained by repression goes astray. The idea capable of life carries itself. Millions of men spontaneously follow it.

Once again, in the course of recent months, have come words of prayer in which both sorrow and pain for the problems of the fatherland have been mingled. What follows are the words that the Holy Father spoke last autumn:

"We include together, in our very profound concern, all those who have been separated from their families, from their daily life, from their work, because of the events surrounding martial law. We are conscious and concerned for the lot of those interned, to whom society and the church can bring some assistance. We are concerned more and more for the lot of prisoners and of those condemned, to whom society and the church have practically no access. We think, with the greatest solicitude, of those who are undertaking hunger strikes in prison. All these brothers and sisters belong to a great national community, just as the six million people who gave their lives during World War II belong to it. The nation has the right and the duty to be concerned with them; it has the right to ask that the rights of man be respected when dealing with prisoners. Aren't we the faithful about whom Christ said: ''I was in prison and you came to me?'' (Matthew 24:36)

The pope further observed, ''Through the truth that comes to us from the cross of Christ, it is necessary to look at all of these crosses in our land. . . . These crosses are numerous; numerous are the persons who have been interned, arrested, condemned. Many have been beaten and ill-treated in their human dignity. Many are the families, many are the local groups that suffer.''

Strengthened by his concern for his native land, for the nation, we will, for a long time, be able to continue heeding, with the greatest respect, the words that the Holy Father pronounced. We are recalling them, not in order to sow disturbance in society, not to play with human feelings. We are recalling these trials of the year that has just passed in order to draw this lesson from them: this seed of concern for our native land, cast in August 1980 upon Polish soil, irrigated with the blood, with the tears, with the suffering, and with the sorrow of our sisters and our brothers in the course of the past year; this sowing of the seed, therefore, must bear good fruit. The powerful tree of freedom and justice must bud forth here. We do not have the right to lose this hope. For there exists in our nation sufficient capacity for active and creative work on behalf of the common good of the fatherland. This nation, which offers its sorrowful experiences to God through the mouth of the Holy Father, this nation is capable of many sacrifices, and still it hopes for real peace and concord. It hopes for the guarantee that these efforts will not once again be for nought. The nation understands better today the words of Norwid: ''It is not necessary to bow before the inevitable and leave truth behind the door.'' It is not necessary to bow before the inevitable. . . .

Let us pray to the Mother of God, she who has given God to the world, that in our fatherland all people of good-will will be able to build a future based upon the principles of justice, love, goodness, and peace and upon the solidarity of hearts and of human spirits.

Our Lady of Jasna Gora, you know better than anyone how millions of Polish hearts are passionately concerned with truth, with responsibility, with freedom and with love. Welcome the cry of these hearts and grant that the forces of good may bring about victory in this country that for centuries, has considered you its Mother and its Queen. Amen.

Prayer of the Faithful
Let us pray for:
—the Holy Father, John Paul II: that he may come to visit his fatherland and confirm us in the hope of justice and of real liberty;
—our country: that the basic rights of man be respected in it;
—arrested, condemned, and interned persons: that they be given again the liberty, unjustly taken from them, and that they be permitted to work effectively for the welfare of the fatherland;
—those who have been dismissed from their jobs and their families: grant them, in a special way, your pro-

tection;

—our brothers who have lost their lives or their health during this state of war: that their sacrifice and their suffering might become a sea of genuine solidarity of human hearts;

—those who govern us: that they remember that only the power given by the people is sacred;

—the media: that they not be used for the lie and for instigating trouble in society;

—those who serve the lie and injustice: help them, Lord, to see the reality of their self-humiliation;

—those who, against their will, are celebrating these feasts away from their households: that their pain contribute to affirming and strengthening love for the fatherland;

—all of us gathered together here in prayer: that we cultivate, with courage and without fear, the ideals for which we have struggled in the ranks of Solidarity;

—artists and all intellectuals: that they not be lacking strength in the fight for the dignity and freedom of our nation.

We pray you, hear us, O Lord!

My dear son,
Here today are my best wishes for Christmas,
for you and for those who share your lot,
everywhere, wherever you find yourselves. I appeal to
your hearts.
Very dear ones, it is my heart which speaks to you.
My best wishes reach you in the penitentiaries,
throughout Poland in which you are imprisoned.
Have this lively sentiment: all of us are with you.
There is no forgetting.
Solidarity lives in our hearts and in our minds.
The best of it will always remain
and nothing will be able to destroy it,
neither bludgeon nor prison, nor repression, nor perse-

cution.
Yes, those who have condemned you deceive themselves!
Let them hear then, each of them,
what a wise man who was a prisoner says to them:
The body, you can imprison, the mind, never!
No one can lock up the lofty thought of man,
neither the heart which suffers for its native land,
nor the faith of the ancients, nor the expectation of children,
nor the feelings which show the unity of a people.
They become strong and powerful
to crack the bars and throw down the walls.
They climb up to heaven in order to strengthen our hope,
like the lark which sings unceasingly about the splendor of the sun.
May they not come to lack either simple solidarity
or faith! And the Lord will say: Let Poland be!
Let it be born of its sorrow, of its sacrifice, of its tears, of its blood,
and of its misery and its humiliation.
Yes, this will be our resurrection!
May God have you in His protective custody and may He watch over your health.

(Letter from a mother to her son condemned to eight years in prison during the state of war)

Before the Blessing

I would like to thank, with all my heart, those who pray for the intentions of the fatherland and those who suffer the most for it. We all know how greatly the fatherland today has need of this prayer and the blessing of God.

I particularly thank again the artists. And above all, you, dear actors, for having helped us during this year of martial law to give a greater quality and depth to our prayer for the fatherland. You have given renditions in our midst of the patriotic and religious words of Polish poetry.

During this long year, you have been absent from our homes.[1] But your long absence from radio and television and your unfailing attitude of solidarity with those who are undergoing suffering for our fatherland are, for us, a symbol of the struggle for the common good, for justice, for true liberty.

It is because of your attitude that you have become closer to us and dearer to our hearts and our consciences. We cordially thank those who are present here and, through your good offices, we thank all those who preserve the dignity of those who playact. May God be with you!

---

[1] Allusion to the boycott of official means of communication, led by Polish artists.

1983

JANUARY 1983

Before Holy Mass
...In the past, Polish kings begged You
in Holy Czestochowa,
to give them back the people.
In the past, before dying,
Poland, still great and intact,
had chosen You for her Queen.
In the past, this Nation has served You with its
weapons
Leading the battle of Christ against the pagans.
Queen of Poland, Duchess of Lithuania,
Have pity on us.

The world is full of suffering, of punishments, of
torments,
Of fear and of sorrow, You see, Our Lady,
what attracts and what wounds the heart
On the grave strewn field of this life.
You know from what souls are dying.
Cause there to shine forth a ray of Your wondrous
heaven
upon the ruins of hearts and of dead people,
You who reign at the pinnacle of the universe,
Have pity on us.

(Zygmunt Krasinski, The Prayer)

Introduction to the Liturgy
In the autumn of 1861 Archbishop Antoni Fijalkowski, on his deathbed, pronounced these words: "Stay always with the nation. Try, insofar as your capacity as shepherds of the people allows, to defend the cause of the common fatherland, and never forget that you are Poles." By the

common prayer for the fatherland and those who are suffering for it, we are fulfilling in some way the will of this great pastor whom God called to Himself. As in the case of the difficult times before the January uprising, the 120th anniversary of which we are celebrating, we want these solemn masses for the fatherland to maintain a spirit of patriotic love in us so that they enkindle hope and increase our pain-filled longing for the welfare of our common house. They must help us to draw from the treasure of our hearts what has most value, namely every good that will help us to conquer evil.

Reading: Proverbs 2:1–15
My son, if you take my words to heart, if you set store by my commandments,
turning your ear to wisdom, and applying your heart to truth:
yes, if your plea is for clear perception, if you cry out for discernment,
if you look for it as if it were silver, and search for it as for buried treasure,
you will then understand what the fear of Yahweh is, and discover the knowledge of God.
For Yahweh himself is giver of wisdom, from his mouth issues knowledge and discernment.

He keeps his help for honest men, he is the shield of those whose ways are honourable;
he stands guard over the paths of justice, he keeps watch on the way of his devoted ones.
Then you will understand what virtue is, justice, and fair dealing, all paths that lead to happiness.

When wisdom comes into your heart and knowledge is a delight to you,
then prudence will be there to watch over you, and

discernment be your guardian
to keep you from the way that is evil, from the man
whose speech is deceitful,
from those who leave the paths of honesty to walk the
roads of darkness:
men who find their joy in doing wrong, and their
delight in deceitfulness,
whose tracks are twisted, and the paths that they tread
crooked.

Meditation Song: Psalm 56:2–7, 11–12
Take pity on me, God, as they harry me,
pressing their attacks home all day.
All day my opponents harry me,
hordes coming in to the attack.

Raise me up when I am most afraid,
I put my trust in you;
in God, whose word I praise,
in God I put my trust, fearing nothing;
what can men do to me?

All day long they twist what I say,
all they think of is how to harm me,
they conspire, lurk, spy on my movements,
determined to take my life.

In God whose word I praise,
in Yahweh, whose word I praise,
in God I put my trust, fearing nothing;
what can man do to me?

Gospel: Luke 20:17–26
   But he looked hard at them and said, 'Then what does
this text in the scriptures mean:

It was the stone rejected by the builders that became the keystone?

Anyone who falls on that stone will be dashed to pieces; anyone it falls on will be crushed.'

But for their fear of the people, the scribes and the chief priests would have liked to lay hands on him that very moment, because they realized that this parable was aimed at them.

So they waited their opportunity and sent agents to pose as men devoted to the Law, and to fasten on something he might say and so enable them to hand him over to the jurisdiction and authority of the governor. They put to him this question, 'Master, we know that you say and teach what is right; you favour no one, but teach the way of God in all honesty. Is it permissible for us to pay taxes to Caesar or not?' But he was aware of their cunning and said, 'Show me a denarius. Whose head and name are on it?' 'Caesar's' they said. 'Well then,' he said to them 'give back to Caesar what belongs to Caesar—and to God what belongs to God.'

As a result, they were unable to find fault with anything he had to say in public; his answer took them by surprise and they were silenced.

Before the Homily

Beautiful and invincible is human solidarity.
Neither treason, nor the lie, nor the arm loaded with repression,
nor the opinion of research, nor the government edict (ukase) will break her tender bonds.
It is she who opens the chains and joins hands together.
And the uninhabited nests with palms of welcome,
she fills up for the return of the wounded bird,
or, even still, with a quill which will make note of the

testament of fidelity.
She transforms the river of tears into an ocean of
Hope,
she snaps her fingers to choose from among the broad
list of the lost.
Accomplice of man's lot, sister of our misery,
also as steadfast in sorrow,
as impatient for the joy which she wishes to share.
What she binds for all time,
no things nor anyone will ever be able to separate:
neither the lousiest type of meanness nor greatest
dread nor the cross of bars nor bitterness of exile.
She guides the life rafts of those who have escaped
once more toward the ports of freedom.
She does not know deserted islands on the ocean.
She cuts through the icy archipelagoes by means of
warm currents.
Her hand is tender in dressing wounds,
strong and careful in protecting the downtrodden,
in order to give to the famished the last bit of bread.
Determined, she signs with her surname and given
name, she signs for lost causes.
In the name of Good, of Truth which despite every-
thing . . . will conquer.

(T. Szyma, Axioms)

Homily

From the beginning of our history, our ancestors have poured forth their blood in order to prevent a foreign enemy from depriving us of the highest national value, our freedom.

For "the struggle for freedom, when it is begun with the blood of the father, falls like an inheritance upon the son."

Poles have known how to defend the fatherland before the invader; they have known how to demand a genuine, complete, and total freedom for her during the Partition period. They have always been accompanied by the light of the Gospel of Christ: freedom is a gift of God himself. There have been many uprisings and national revolutions. The insurrections of November 1830 and January 1863 deserve special attention since both, in comparison with what we are living through today, were quite similar to our present situation.

First of all, then, a few words about the revolution of 1830: it was primarily the work of youth who refused to accept the situation imposed on Poland by the great powers. The patriotic spirit of young lads from the school for cadets made Warsaw a revolutionary center. Unfortunately, the power remained in the hands of people who had made for themselves quite a good situation—people who were paid with money from the occupier. These folks did not in any way help the revolutionaries. They placed in the government some persons who enjoyed the high regard of our patriots; this was done only to deceive the public. The uprising was squelched, but the will for independence remained.

For "the struggle for freedom, when it is begun with the blood of the father falls like an inheritance upon the son."

The year 1863! Let us attempt to imagine the situation, the ambiance, and some of the causes that impelled our ancestors to get themselves ready for a struggle against various odds on a winter evening, January 22, 1863.

After twenty-five years, martial law decreed on the occasion of the November Insurrection was lifted in 1856. The situation was undoubtedly less black than in 1830, but the feeling of the people was more lively—it often happens when a nation has suffered without recrimination and seems to be insensitive to the most humiliating decrees—when their yoke became lighter, they went about violently shaking off that yoke.

When the evil that was accepted as something inde-
structible becomes totally incompatible with the idea of
freeing oneself completely, a moral revolution begins in
society. Christian values, often proclaimed, but only
proclaimed *so far*, become the basis of life among wider
and wider circles of the society. In great numbers, people gather in the churches. They solemnly celebrate anniversaries about which it was previously necessary to be
silent. After holy mass at the Carmelite Church on the occasion of the thirtieth anniversary of the November Insurrection, those who were there were called upon to return
once again that evening; spontaneously, thousands of
Warsaw citizens responded. When a particular sign was
given, despite the mud, the people got down on their
knees right on the pavement and sang with tears in their
eyes: "0 God, protect Poland."

These patriotic sentiments were being developed; the
people took seriously to heart the appeal: "God, protect
our fatherland." The patriotic sentiments were then
manifested on different occasions. Nevertheless, the
authorities either did not understand these sentiments that
were stirring up society or did not wish to understand
them. For them, anything that took place in Poland was
the result of foreign agitation and interference. For the regime, accustomed to law and order in society, this
avalanche of patriotic manifestations came as a tremendous shock and surprise. They decided to use force. On
February 27, 1861, at the exit of the Leszno church, fifty-
five rifle shots were fired. Five men fell dead and fifteen
persons were wounded.

The patriotism of the nation, however, was motivat-
ed by a real concern for restoring complete independence
to the fatherland. The nation did not want confrontation.
Despite this tragedy, they sought an agreement with the
regime that was at the service of the occupier. This was
clear in the request sent to the czar. Margrave Wielopol-

ski, a Pole, was called to the government. He obviously enjoyed the full confidence of Petersburg. To some, he represented a providential man, a great statesman; to others he was a traitor and a renegade from the beginning. Unfortunately, the facts quickly proved the latter understanding of his services to be correct. As if he were doing it deliberately, he aroused the hostility of the population. The reforms that he attempted to introduce were rejected. Then the regime abolished all forms of self-governing organizations, which had been created on the occasion called "The Polish Days" and which had acquired authority and support in society.

Once again there were innocent victims. The nation was more and more humiliated. Street demonstrations ceased; no longer were patriotic emblems carried or worn. In appearance all was calm, but this was only an illusion. This situation did not last. Patriotism was manifested in churches, and the efforts designed to lead the bishops to put an end to these manifestations ended in failure.

The demonstration that accompanied Archbishop Fijalkowski's funeral and the announcement of a demonstration on the anniversary of the death of Tadeus Kosciuszko furnished the motive for the restoration of martial law on October 14. On the one hand some draconian measures and on the other hand, some crooked promises to lift the state of siege in response to a submissive attitude were designed to calm the overflowing spirits of the population. That was indeed how the authorities had calculated, but they were deceived. The next day the people went back into the churches by the thousands. When the forbidden hymn was intoned, the soldiers were given the order to surround the churches. That night, at the instigation of the governor general who hated Poles, it was decided to seize the churches by force. Some drunk and "trigger-happy" soldiers threw themselves upon the praying people. 1,687 men were arrested. In Warsaw, patrols of Cossacks struck down every passerby whom they met.

The restoration of martial law and the incidents of October 15 served to convince even those who had previously hoped to find compromises that agreement with the authorities was no longer possible. Wielopolski, operating out of an almost pathological blindness, was unwilling to understand that vengeance and rigidity do not pay in politics—even his admirer Przyborski maintained that a government that forces its subjects to loyalty by decrees ceases to be a government.

Finally, on the winter evening of January 22, 1863, the people rose in an armed revolution. Despite its failure, the uprising notably swelled the circle of Poles who were becoming conscious of the heritage of their ancestors and of their national aspiration. This was the seed thrown on Polish soil. And this aspiration for independence remains in their consciences.

For "the struggle for freedom, once begun with the blood of the father falls like an inheritance upon the son."

Then came World War I. In the last two hundred years, this was the only war that Poland won, a war after which there was neither a regime nor a power imposed upon it. And when, a short time after, this real freedom was threatened from the east, the entire nation mobilized itself to defend its real freedom.

And it was then that the holy Mother of God showed, in a special manner on her Feast of the Assumption, that she was Queen of Poland. She accomplished a miraculous victory near Warsaw, a victory which remains in th memory of the nation as "the miracle of the Vistula." During the occupation, the people of Warsaw rose up again in the insurrection of the summer of 1944. This insurrection left a great many victims in its wake because the Allies abandoned Warsaw; instead of assisting, they watched as Warsaw agonized and poured out its blood. And the abandoned people of Warsaw offered their best sons on the altar of freedom for the fatherland.

For "the struggle for freedom, once begun with the blood of the father, falls like an inheritance upon the son."

One cay say, as does the poet Jerzy Zagorski, of the streets of Warsaw:

Take in your hand a handful of this earth,
Squeeze it tight, blood will flow from it.
For in this earth, in this clay stained with blood,
Each resting place of the bones of the martyrs,
Is a relic, a golden angel.

The aspiration for freedom was not extinguished after World War II. We know some examples of the nation's stirrings, some stirrings in which it was more a matter of freedom than of daily bread, stirrings to recover human dignity; for these rights were not being respected.

Our late lamented primate, Cardinal Stefan Wyszynski, said in the final year of his life:

The world of work has known several deceptions and many limitations during these last decades. The workers and all of society have experienced in Poland great suffering because of the limitation of rights essential to the human person— limitation of freedom in the area of thought, of vision of the world, of religious faith, of education for youth. All of that was snuffed out. In the area of professional work, there was created a model of man forced to work and be silent. When this repression had sufficiently exasperated everyone, there was a stirring in behalf of liberty. Solidarity was born.

A contemporary poet has stated,
Never as cruelly
have our backs been flogged
with the stick of the lie and deception as
clearly evident as the fire of mighty furnaces
and the tremendous noise of machines.

Never also have we so clearly seen
the face of treason
gaping between the metallic doors of
extermination.

Freedom is a reality that God has placed in man by creating him in His image and His likeness. A nation possessing a thousand years of Christian tradition will always aspire to total freedom. For it is impossible to beat this aspiration down by repression because repression is the force of someone who does not possess the truth. It is possible to bend man by repression but impossible to make him a slave. A Pole who loves God and the fatherland will lift himself up from every humiliation, because he is kneeling before God. We know so many examples of this from early and contemporary history.

I cite, by way of conclusion to this sermon, the words spoken by our present primate, Cardinal Jozef Glemp, who, last November 7, said at Lublin: "A humiliated nation has the right to protest, has the right to demand its rights . . . It has the right to be itself."

Let us pray today, on this 120th anniversary of the patriotic uprising of insurgents, that we will be able to cultivate the aspiration for true freedom in ourselves, in our families, in our various circles, in our jobs, and in our nation.

Amen.

Prayer of the Faithful

Let us pray for . . .

—the Holy Father, troubled about the lot of our fatherland, that he come to visit his homeland in order to strengthen the hope and resolve of Poles;

—those who have poured out their blood for the fatherland by struggling against the occupier during the January uprising, that God give to them, in payment for their sacrifice, eternal happiness;

—our sisters and brothers who have given their

lives or their health during the state of war, that their
sacrifice and their suffering serve the moral renewal of
the nation;

—those who have been arrested and condemned,
those who have been fired from their jobs, and those
who must hide, that they find in God and man aid and
hope;

—our fatherland, that it may be able to develop
happily in justice and true freedom;

—all those who have sold themselves in the service of the lie, of injustice, and of repression, that God
open their hearts and help them to see the shame of
their own humiliation;

—ourselves, that we do not lose faith in the ideals
for which we have struggled in the ranks of Solidarity.

We pray you, hear us, O Lord.

Prayer After Communion
My Poland is gray,
like the face of a worn-out woman,
without a smile, without hope,
eyes saddened by pain.

My Poland is lost,
placed at the crossroads,
bearing the cross of suffering on her shoulders,
sorrowful as at Golgotha.

My Poland is frightened,
without bread, without truth,
worthy of the highest sentiments
but bearing the burden of a foreign shame

My Poland is in tears,
your mothers weep over the graves,

You look, clothed with black
all the way down the covered cross.

My Poland is anxious
about the lot of your thousand sons
imprisoned and exiled,
dispersed throughout the world.

My Poland is in prayer
to remain Polish;
with Mary in her Churches,
May you welcome Your tormented Nation.

(Teresa, "My Poland")

To live without knowing that your country is a slave?
To live and to feign living in freedom?
Not to see the tears and the sorrowful sufferings?
To remain deaf, dumb, and blind?
To live in hovels and to construct palaces?
To be married and to live separated?
To be humiliated?
To live without knowing what freedom is in the
world?
To think ceaselessly and secretly of money?
Without seeing the sun and having the eyes of a bat?
Having only one thing which counts: to have your gut
filled?
To pay with gratitude for unceasing torment?
To live and work for the enemy under the rod?
And each day to fear the true word?
To live in makeshift skins?
Without seeing the truth?
Without thinking?
More freedom, More warmth!
Advance toward the light, advance toward the sun!
Let each hold a torch of clear fire!

Let each flame be a burning fear!
If you do not groan, if you act,
If you remember, you are a man!
Enough of living humbly,
It would be better to burn,
You must set yourself ablaze—if you are a man!
                    (S. Krawanski,
             "Reflections on the Holocaust,"
                    Wolodymir, 1969

FEBRUARY 1983

I welcome you all, dear brothers and sisters to our monthly holy mass for the fatherland. I greet, in an especially warm way, those who have just arrived from distant regions of our country in order to participate in this common prayer. For one month straight, from my bed of suffering in the hospital, I have accompanied you in prayer. Today we are going to pray together, to pray that God take pity on our tormented fatherland.

Several of you have commented about these words *Poland in Need* printed on the trucks that are transporting nourishment, clothing, and medication for our country from aboard. People from around the world are aiding "Poland in Need" in order to lessen our material misery. But we are also receiving a great number of letters from different churches, from Christians in various countries. They are writing to say that they are praying for us and that they are participating in holy Masses being offered for Poland. This certainly is a very significant and important help from brothers who are sustaining us by their prayer. We are deeply in their debt. Since others are praying for us with fervor, no one should be disturbed by the fact that we, gathered together here, are praying for our fatherland.

I would like to ask this of you: that our prayer sessions take place in a spirit of seriousness and recollection that one thing alone brings us here: the welfare of our fatherland and our common prayer for it. I beg you, therefore, not to hold up, on your own initiative, any banner, flag, or inscriptions either inside or outside the church—no demonstration by chanting, no calls to demonstrate. After the service, let us disperse in a spirit of seriousness and return to our homes. The men in white and blue armbands

are ushers. Please respect their recommendations and
listen to them.

Before Holy Mass
Come down, Spirit of power,
increase our strength
beyond the mind, beyond sentiment,
beyond tears of women and of men.
Increase our strength
beyond the graves of our brothers,
beyond the lamentations of orphans and of widows,
beyond the pleas of those murdered by gas,
beyond the disturbance of sudden bombings,
beyond fear, when one is not ready to die,
and when one desires only the mouth of the beloved.
Look:
submitted to the super-human test,
—hammered down by so much suffering,
we hold our heads up to the annihilation which is
coming.
We struggle for ourselves in the world.
Increase our strength
beyond all martrydom,
beyond fatigue
and cruelty and all the litany of our pains,
Let us clench our teeth,
with rock-like tenacity:
We will not allow to fall from our hands
the standards of the peoples.
Strengthen us up to the very end.
The war, we must win it,
This autumn, this winter,
Or in a matter of years.
Strengthen us beyond life and death!
Come down Spirit of power,

Increase our strength.

(Kazimier Wierzynski,
"Come Down, Spirit of Power,"
September 5, 1939)

Introduction to the Liturgy

We place ourselves before the altar of Christ, gathered together in prayer for the fatherland. Today our thoughts and our hearts go out to all of those of our brothers who are in prison. We are going to pray that all of those falsely condemned recover their freedom. We are going to join our prayer to the appeal of the Polish bishops in behalf of amnesty for our brothers.

Reading: Ephesians 6:10–18

Finally, grow strong in the Lord, with the strength of his power. Put God's armour on so as to be able to resist the devil's tactics. For it is not against human enemies that we have to struggle, but against the Sovereignties and the Powers who originate the darkness in this world, the spiritual army of evil in the heavens. That is why you must rely on God's armour, or you will not be able to put up any resistance when the worst happens, or have enough resources to hold your ground.

So stand your ground, with *truth buckled round your waist*, and *integrity for a breastplate*, wearing for shoes on your feet *the eagerness to spread the gospel of peace* and always carrying the shield of faith so that you can use it to put out the burning arrows of the evil one. And then you must accept *salvation from God to be your helmet* and receive the word of God from the Spirit on every possible occasion. Never get tired of staying awake to pray for all the saints.

Meditation Song: Psalm 94:16–23

No one ever stood up for me against the wicked,

not a soul took a stand to save me from evil men;
without Yahweh's help, I should, long ago,
have gone to the Home of Silence.

I need only say, 'I am slipping,'
and your love, Yahweh, immediately supports me;
and in the middle of all my troubles
you console me and make me happy.

You never consent to that corrupt tribunal
that imposes disorder as law,
that takes the life of the virtuous
and condemns the innocent to death.

No! Yahweh is still my citadel,
my God is a rock where I take shelter;
he will pay them back for all their sins,
he will silence their wickedness,
Yahweh our God will silence them.

Song before the Gospel:
How long, O Lord, how long are the guilty going to continue to boast, spilling forth a flood of words, raising their
cock-sure voices? How long are these malefactors going
to boast?

Gospel: Luke 4:16–21
He came to Nazareth, where he had been brought up,
and went into the synagogue on the sabbath day as he
usually did. He stood up to read and they handed him the
scroll of the prophet Isaiah. Unrolling the scroll he found
the place where it is written:
The spirit of the Lord has been given to me,
for he has anointed me.
He has sent me to bring the good news to the
poor,

to proclaim liberty to captives
and to the blind new sight,
to set the downtrodden free,
to proclaim the Lord's year of favour.

He then rolled up the scroll, gave it back to the assistant and sat down. And all eyes in the synagogue were fixed on him. Then he began to speak to them, "This text is being fulfilled today even as you listen."

Homily

In the person of Jesus Christ the words of the prophet Isaiah, recalled in the passage of the gospel that we have just read, are truly fulfilled.

"He has sent me to bring good news to the poor, to announce to captives freedom, and to the blind their return to sight, to grant liberty to the oppressed, to proclaim a year of favor of the Lord."

Throughout all of his active ministry, Jesus Christ wanted people to understand that they were created for freedom, for the freedom of the children of God. Throughout his earthly life, Christ wanted to help people to understand the meaning and the value of human life, the meaning and the value of suffering. Because of miracles accomplished by his divine power, he had diminished physical and spiritual sufferings. He had wanted to make people aware of the suffering of others.

God created man free so that man could accept God or reject him. Love would not exist if we were forced to love.

Whence then, throughout the world, do slavery and prisons come?

There exist some invisible prisons. They are very numerous. Some people are born, grow up, and die in such prisons. There is the prison that certain systems and regimes establish. These prisons are not content with destroying the body. They go much further. They seek out the soul. They attack true freedom.

Man has also constructed some prisons in brick and mortar. Some prisons are surrounded by barbed wire and by walls.

And since man has destroyed the system of values intended by God, these prisons are sometimes necessary.

Nevertheless, it is not good that prison walls serve to shut up men because they think differently, feel differently, or work in other ways for the good of the fatherland.

As early as 1968 the Polish bishops declared,
No one should be declared an enemy becuase of
his opinions. To consider, as enemies, those who
search for good is not to serve social morality,
rather it is to deprive the nation of numerous tal-
ents, gifts, and initiatives which can contribute
to the enrichment of social life in various sectors.

These words of the bishops seem to us today to have particular, current relevance. For in our fatherland at the present time, many, condemned or waiting to be judged, are being held in prisons. They are in prison because they always wanted and continue to want the welfare of the fatherland. They were following their personal convictions, convictions common to millions of Poles.

In his prayer to our Lady of Jasna Gora during the period of martial law, Pope John Paul II cried out, on more than one occasion: "Mother, I beg You, give freedom once again to all those who are unjustly deprived of it."

Likewise, the bishops on more than one occasion have expressed the hope that "the state of war might quickly end and that those interned might be released, and that those condemned for activities connected with martial law be granted amnesty."

At the end of last year, despite efforts undertaken by the bishops, those interned were released—not as a result of the appeal of the bishops—but because of a newly created organization. Two months have rolled by since, and it is always difficult for us to understand why, on Christmas Eve, certain of our brothers saw their internment transformed into arrest. Why have they had to wait more than one year in a camp of internment in order to learn that they were accused of deeds that they had not committed? Isn't this really a matter of a symbolic action against the whole of Solidarity?

Christ is especially present in the midst of those who suffer. He identifies himself with them when he says "I was in prison and you came to visit me . . .; I was hungry and you gave me to eat."

Is Christ not in a special way with those who, behind the bars of the prison at Rakowiecka, wrote these words to their wives or sisters: "Don't do anything for me. Know that I am capable of enduring everything that I have to. I beg you to preserve unshakeable faith in divine providence and to behave as a noble human being who is a Pole. Prove your courage, pray for the cause and for me, pray to our Lady of Czestochowa." These are the words of one of the imprisoned members of Solidarity. Only a man, faithful to his ideals, faithful to his conscience, can think, feel, and write in this manner.

If, then, from behind prison bars, our brothers can breathe into the hearts of their relatives confidence and faith in God and fidelity to the common cause, how much more ought we to do, we who have the possiblity of committing our energies and our hearts to the welfare of others!

Are we well aware that these brothers, condemned by virtue of the decree regarding martial law, our brothers for whom the bishops asked amnesty some weeks ago, have defended the dignity of the workers and that they want to remain faithful to the ideals and the hopes that millions of people made their own back in 1980?

How very important it is for them and for us to know that the mutual solidarity of human hearts continues, that their sufferings are our own!

May their families be showered with material and spiritual aid! May we, each day in our homes at evening prayer, pray to God for the innocent who have been in prison, asking for them the strength to keep looking forward to freedom. May we pray for ourselves and may we teach our children to pray for our ideals and for national and patriotic initiatives.

Satan will continue to reenforce his empire on earth and in our fatherland, the kingdom of the lie, of hatred, of fear, unless we each day become stronger by the grace of God and unless we reach out with shared sorrow, heart, and love to our brothers, who suffer innocently in prisons, and to their families.

In certain circles the families of prisoners are accorded assistance and general respect. But there are other circles in which fear is stronger than the meaning of moral duty.

Let us remember the words of Christ: "What you do to the least of my brethren, you do to me."

The bishops demand amnesty and, in the communiqué read today, amnesty includes the liberation of all those who are imprisoned by virtue of the decree of martial law. It is a question of amnesty, of the abolition of martial law, and not of a token gesture, for it is inconceivable that the chains that bind the limbs be removed in order to place them on souls.

Some women imprisoned at Fordon wrote "We want freedom but not at any price. Not at the price of the renunciation of our ideals, not at the price of betraying ourselves and those who have confidence in us."

"Let us place truth above everything," says the poet. "Let us accord life in truth pride of place, if we do not wish our conscience to be stricken with dry rot." The realistic words *life in truth* can cost dearly and sometimes include risks. But as our late lamented primate, Cardinal Stefan Wyszynski stated, "Only the cockle does not demand to be paid. It is sometimes necessary to pay for the grain of wheat of truth.''

Let us not throw away our ideals for a bowl of porridge. Let us not throw away our ideals by selling out our brothers.

That the hour may come in which we will be able to share our daily bread in love and solidarity depends upon you, upon all of us, upon our concern for our innocent imprisoned brothers, upon our life in truth each day.

At this moment, in which our nation has need of all the strength it can muster to recover and preserve its freedom, let us pray God to give us the power of his Spirit and confidence in victory, to soothe our hearts, to enlighten the troubled minds of our brothers, and to awaken in the nation the spirit of true solidarity among human hearts. May they beat with the rhythm of the heart of God who loves us so much.

Prayer before Communion
More often You are outraged,
More grotesquely funny are the crowns placed upon
Your forehead.
More the cry insulting You: show Your Face!
More often are you relegated to a position of fading
footprints on the sands of time.
More regret, scoffing, furor,
(Your word its true—will not displace a rock)
The more I am able to be sure of this truth:
You are the Alpha and the Omega.
(Czeslaw Milosz, 1969, translation by Krzysztof Jezewski and Dominic Sila, in *Poems* 1934–1982, Luneau Ascot Ed., Paris, 1984)

Before the Blessing
We reiterate our demand to leave the church after holy mass and to return to your homes in calm and recollection. Let us be courageous.

MARCH 1983

Solemn Entrance in procession after the blessing of the cross and of the palms

Reading: 2 Corinthians 6:2–10

For he says: *At the favourable time, I have listened to you; on the day of salvation I came to your help.* Well, now is the favourable time; this is the day of salvation.

We do nothing that people might object to, so as not to bring discredit on our function as God's servants. Instead, we prove we are servants of God by great fortitude in times of suffering: in times of hardship and distress; when we are flogged, or sent to prison, or mobbed; labouring, sleepless, starving. We prove we are God's servants by our purity, knowledge, patience, and kindness; by a spirit of holiness, by a love free from affectation; by the word of truth and by the power of God; by being armed with the weapons of righteousness in the right hand and in the left prepared for honour or disgrace, for blame or praise; taken for impostors while we are genuine; obscure yet famous; said to be dying and here are we alive; rumoured to be executed before we are sentenced; thought most miserable and yet we are always rejoicing; taken for paupers though we make others rich, for people having nothing though we have everything.

Gospel: Luke 23:1–49
Narrative of the Passion of Jesus Christ

Homily

Holy Mass is the most perfect form of prayer that the faithful address to God, Father of nations and of peoples.

By our prayer, we want to serve God and mankind. We wish to join God to the difficult and sorrowful problems of our fatherland.

To serve God is to search out the path of human hearts. To serve God is to speak of evil as a sickness for which we one day, absolutely, need to find a cure. To serve God is to point out and brand evil and all its manifestations.

The readings that we have just heard regarding the martyrdom and death of our Savior show to what point Christ had to suffer, how many humiliations he had to undergo—from those who did not want to accept the words of truth that he brought to them—from those who condemned him to an unjust death by means of crucifixion. Such was the price paid by Christ for his love and devotion on behalf of the welfare of humankind. But we have forgotten it; we did not wish to understand it: we can crucify Love and Truth, but it is impossible to kill them. Down there, on the cross, Truth and Love triumphed over evil, hatred, and death.

We are the disciples of Christ and we know to what point the lack of truth, the triumph of hatred in our Fatherland, impedes the mutual construction of our family home, the dialogue and peace between brothers.

In the course of the Mass that he celebrated in the capital of El Salvador, the Holy Father declared:

> The lie is tactically used against dialogue, this lie which abuses man, which utilizes false propaganda, which fuels aggression. Dialogue becomes unfruitful when the parties give themselves over to idealogies which are contrary to human dignity, which see, in struggle, the motivating force of history, in force the source of truth, and consider the first rule of politics to be dividing the citizenry into two groups— friends and enemies. Dialogue is not a tactical

ploy but a sincere effort to find a response and to bring about peace and concord in the midst of the sufferings, misery and weariness of the multitides who are hungering for peace.

The problem on which we must reflect together today is exceptionally difficult, but now is the time to do it. Two days ago, the Holy Father opened the Holy Year, the year of redemption and of reconciliation.

He does so no doubt because the great majority of the population is looking for this redemption, this reconciliation built upon proper foundations.

In the beginning of martial law, the bishops of Poland called for a social compact, but from the beginning they clearly fixed the conditions for this. They have condemned, with clear determination, everything that hinders this agreement.

Thus, since December 15, 1981, the bishops have stated that the decision of the authorities to inaugurate martial law was a blow to social hope, which was waiting for a solution to the problems of the fatherland by means of an agreement.

The bishops firmly demanded a dialogue, necessary for excluding every radical approach that could result in the loss of health or human life.

On several occasions they recalled that the Solidarity union, which defends the rights of workers, is indispensable to the restoration of peace and harmony in society.

Last February they specified that the parties to the agreement ought to be the regime and the representatives of Solidarity, which enjoys such widespread approval in society.

When, by the illegal act of October 8, 1982, the union organizations, suspended up until that time, were dissolved, the primate of Poland declared, in his talk at

Niepokalanow, that because of the discussion with the working class to which the Church is closely bound, the most important element of social identity had been suppressed; and that by abolishing the legal existence of this important partner in authentic dialogue, the Solidarity unimportant partner in authentic dialogue, the Solidarity union organization had been dealt a grievous blow, which is being felt by all of society.

the excesses brought by the regime against those being interned at Kwidzyn, as well as the attempts to place perfectly healthy people in psychiatric institutions.

The Church vigorously condemned the pressures that were brought to bear upon people, by force, to obain the signing of declarations that were contrary to their consciences.

Thus, on the one hand, the church branded repression or evil while, on the other hand, it called for a social compact or agreement for peace and harmony and for dialogue.

What is it that today still hinders peace and concord? What is it that serves it?

Many among those who are present in this church could cite a whole series of reasons that still make this national peace and harmony difficult.

It is certainly not the bitterness derived from powerlessness and humiliation and experienced each day by our brothers and sisters that can serve this peace and harmony.

The trials of representatives demoncratically elected from among the workers cannot serve peace and harmony. If they are at fault, let them stand up and give an answer to those who have placed their confidence in them—those who elected them.

It is not the prison detention of so many of our brothers and sisters because of differences in opinion that can serve this peace and harmony, nor is it anything that results from this detention: The expectation of children whose mothers or fathers are in prison, the tears of women awaiting the return of their husbands and those of mothers who await the return of their sons, broken families, their uncertainties and torments.

Neither can the raids organized against those who, in a spirit of recollection, are returning to their homes after having attended patriotic Masses serve peace and harmony.

Nor can the shows of force in the vicinity of Churches filled with the faithful at prayer serve peace and harmony any more than the activities of troubled workers near the Churches can—these occurred last month in our neighborhood.

Nor is the constant lack of the wherewithal needed by youth to form their personalities according to principles that they have chosen, together with their desire to enter into social life through youth organizations corresponding to their own conceptions of life, conducive to bringing about peace and harmony.

It is not the screening of articles in the Catholic press, such as *Tygodnik Powszechny, Gosc Niedzielny, Niedziela,* by means of the censorship existing during martial law that contributes to peace and harmony.

Neither are the letters, signed by the heads of personnel offices, announcing that the salary of an active member of Solidarity will doubled if he is willing to establish a new union at his place of employment; not to mention the immediate shift to an inferior post, in a job at the other end of Warsaw, imposed on an active member of Solidarity who, out of loyalty to his conscience, refuses to comply. These tactics do not serve peace and harmony!

What I am describing here is not meddling with politics. It is merely a report of the suffering of a father with a large family, who is anxious for the well-being of his own children.

And the examples are many. It is important to recall

all of these wounds inflicted on the nation; it is important to sit together around a table in order to seek solutions.

Personal harmony pursues but one end: the welfare of the fatherland and respect for human dignity.

It is important to extend the hand for peace and harmony in a spirit of love but also in a spirit of justice, as the Holy Father recalled five years ago: love cannot exist without justice. Love surpasses justice but, at the same time, it finds its authenticity through justice.

The nation wants harmony, an agreement, but it wishes guarantees and not just further declarations. It wishes to have a guarantee that it will not be deceived once again, that its pain and its labor will not be in vain. The nation wants harmony that is not a surrender, a renunciation of ideals, aspirations, or faith in a better and more worthy future.

May Holy Week and Easter be a time for prayer for us who offer the crosses of our suffering, the crosses of our salvation—signs of the victory of good over evil, of life over death, of love over hatred.

And for you, brothers, who experience in your hearts a real hatred for the hirelings, may this be a time for reflecting on the fact that force cannot conquer, even if it does triumph for a while. We have the best proof of this at the foot of the cross of Christ. Down there, also, there was repression, there was hatred of the truth. But force and hatred have been conquered by Christ's act of love.

Let us then be powerful in love by praying for our wayward brothers without condemning anyone but by branding and unmasking the evil.

Like true faithful, let us pray with the words of Christ, with the words that he pronounced on the cross: "Father, forgive them, for they do not know what they are doing." And grant us, O Christ, more sensitivity to the power of love than to that of oppression and hatred.

Amen.

Prayer of the Faithful

Let us pray . . .

—for the Church of Christ, that it show to manind the way of truth, of goodness, of love, and of justice;

—for the Holy Father, John Paul II, that despite all obstacles he may come to the fatherland and that he may build up a solidarity of minds and hearts throughout the nation;

—for the families of the condemned, of prisoners, of those in hiding, of those dismissed from their jobs, that they find aid and understanding;

—for the authorities, that they understand that to govern really means to serve in a spirit of love and of justice;

—for those who have been deprived of life during the state of war, that they find a special place in the heavenly kingdom;

—for those who sell themselves to the service of lies, injustice, and repression, that they understand the sorry state of their humiliation;

—that a true harmony in a spirit of fraternity and love be established in our fatherland, that it rid itself of anger, hatred, repression, and humiliation of human dignity;

—that all of the innocent who have been arrested and condemned recover their freedom;

—that we never abandon the ideals for which we have struggled in the ranks of Solidarity

Hear us, O Lord.

Prayer after Communion

Do not cry, Mother, I will return,
do not cry Mother, that serves no purpose,
Bring only into my cell
a bit of bread which feels good,
bring me only the image

of the Most Blessed Virgin Mary,
I will place it near my bunk,
it will warm my frigid mornings.

Bring me, Mother, hope.
Dry your eyes, put on your smile again,
I don't want my prison guard
to see you in tears.
Let him see you happy
for having such a son.
Bring me, Mother, your heart,
Do not weep, wipe your face.

One day, evil will pass away,
Poland will once again be free,
Do not cry, Mother, come to see me
and listen to my words,
I will tell you nothing new,
I will survive the pain and sorrow,
I will not sell my head so cheaply,
God will help me,
for there are thousands
worse off than I.
Do not cry, Mother, come to see me.
Mother, wipe away your bitter tears.

(Otto, "Do Not Cry, Mother")

Into this Country, in which we gather from the soil,
a little bit of bread, because we consider it the gift of
heaven,
we will no longer return there
for the laws of the Fatherland and of heaven have been
overthrown.
No longer is this the same Country and horror reigns
there.
The boots trample over the bread.

But a country so sorrowfully changed,
there is our place of refuge, there is our confidence.
You who overturn the laws and the thrones,
grant that our house will once again become our own.

Hear us, O Lord.

In this Country in which it is a great sin,
to destroy a nest of storks on a pear tree,
recall those who have left
like birds chased by the storm;
it is our fault.
Give us our ancient language, give our venerable
country to those
who have been repressed and despised.
Let their nest await them, all fit and ready,
for it is the same law for the bird as for man.
Let us pray, that this separation be pardoned us
and may it be that our house remain their own.

Hear us, O Lord.

O, this Country
in which we were the first to greet you in years gone
by
Today God is no longer distinguished from Satan.
Today we applaud the one who governs
and the one who bent and crushed moves forward
we pay him with lies, with spite, with contempt.
In order that we might know how to choose between
God and Satan,
make us go through the fire, if need be.
Because we bend ourselves even before You,
Grant that our house become Your own.

Hear us, O Lord.

(Anonymous)

Before the Blessing

We remind you that all the holy Masses for the fatherland have been celebrated in our Church since October 1980 on the last Sunday of each month. By posting false information, some people have attempted to indicate other dates. We therefore state that there will be no other announcement in the city of our holy masses; all the other announcements should be considered acts of provocation. Our holy Masses for the fatherland will always be celebrated on the last Sunday of each month, in April, in May, and the months following.

We call upon the faithful to ignore the troublemakers in our midst who attempt to get us to demonstrate or to chant. Let us agree that after the celebration only the provokers are going to sing and shout in front of the church. By remaining calm and being masters of ourselves, we will see how many there are and who they are. Let us show proof of maturity; let us allow the troublemakers to go away disappointed.

And you, brothers, who have come here on the orders of others, if you want to serve truth and your own dignity, allow the faithful to leave calmly for their homes.

APRIL 1983

It seems useless for me to recall what our conduct should be during our holy Mass for the fatherland, especially after the celebration, all the more so since last month this conduct was perfect and the good order of our church service didn't have to be interrupted.

As a matter of precaution I would like to recall certain guidelines for those who perhaps have not yet participated in our masses.

First of all, we actively participate in holy Mass in order to pray with the greatest fervor and to beg God to have mercy on our fatherland. Finally, we comport ourselves calmly and worthily in Church and also outside of it. Let us pay attention to the recommendations of the ushers who today are wearing on their chests the insignia of our Lady of Czestochowa holding the infant Jesus. Do not pay attention to those who wear other insignia or, for example, university caps. We do not raise our voices, scream, or yell; we do not break into song outside of Church after the end of holy mass. There are no demonstrations; we do not pay attention to troublemakers. If we are attacked or disturbed by whomever the aggressors may be, we do not respond. Stand steadfast like rocks before every external sign of disorder. We do not accept tracts, and we do not hand them out. I beg you once more to remain calm and serious and to pray with fervor.

Introduction to the Liturgy

Each month we stand before Christ in order to serve our fatherland through prayer. We bear in our hearts the most difficult problems of our native land. We bear all of those who suffer for justice: those who have been arrested, especially those who have been arrested this past month, those who are unjustly condemned, those in hiding who want to preserve their dignity and their freedom of conscience, those who have been dismissed from their jobs, all of those whose human dignity is compromised in various ways, and our dear brothers in the National Committee of Solidarity who maintain a healthy attitude in prison and who remain faithful to their and our ideals.

We pray especially for the steelworkers of Warsaw who, two years ago, had the flag of Solidarity blessed here; that flag has been and will always be the expression of hope for freedom, justice, and responsibility and love for the fatherland. We pray, therefore, St. Florian, patron of steelworkers, for help in keeping all these ideals alive in their hearts, so that they can in the near future become once again a reality before which hatred and repression will kneel and so that everyone in our fatherland may live and work in dignity.

Reading: 2 Thessalonians 2:13–17

But we feel that we must be continually thanking God for you, brothers whom the Lord loves, because God chose you from the beginning to be saved by the sanctifying Spirit and by faith in the truth. Through the Good News that we brought he called you to this so that you should share the glory of our Lord Jesus Christ. Stand firm, then, brothers, and keep the traditions that we taught you, whether by word of mouth or by letter. May our Lord Jesus Christ himself, and God our Father who has given us his love and, through his grace, such inexhaustible comfort and such sure hope, comfort you and strengthen you in everything good that you do or say.

Song before the Gospel:
We praise you, O Father, Lord of heaven and of earth, for you have revealed to the simple the mysteries of the kingdom.

Gospel: Matthew 11:25–30

At that time Jesus exclaimed, 'I bless you, Father, Lord of heaven and of earth, for hiding these things from the learned and the clever and revealing them to mere children. Yes, Father, for that is what it pleased you to do. Everything has been entrusted to me by my Father; and no one knows the Son except the Father, just as no one knows the Father except the Son and those to whom the Son chooses to reveal him.

Come to me, all you who labour and are overburdened, and I will give you rest. Shoulder my yoke and learn from me, for I am gentle and humble in heart, *and you will find rest for your souls.* Yes, my yoke is easy and my burden light.'

Homily

The words of the gospel that we have just heard refer in a special way to people who work hard. "Come to me, all you who labour and are overburdened, and I will give you rest." People who work hard have a special need for their hard work, their endurance, and their sweat that pours out to be truly appreciated.

Work is an inseparable companion to man. It is made to serve man, to ennoble him. Man must not be a slave to work, and we must not see in man values that are purely economical. One cannot build his personal, social, and professional life solely upon work. The material cannot count for more than the spiritual side of man. Back in 1904, Stanislaus Witkiewicz asked "What is the strength of the nation—material wealth or great ideas?" And he answered, "Each time that great ideas, great designs for high and far-off goals disappear from the life of the nation, societies break up into little groups acting only in behalf of their own self-interest. They break up into petty societies running after shabby goals." The more society is divided, the easier it is to dominate it, to manipulate it. We all

know the maxim: divide and conquer. It is easy to divide
society when there is a lack of balance between material
and spiritual realities in the life of the citizenry.

By working, man is to ennoble matter, but he must
ennoble himself through work. Indeed, as Pope Pius XI
wrote in the *Encyclical Quadragesimo Anno:* "Matter
comes forth ennobled from the workshop of the craftsman,
while man goes forth from it degraded and downtrodden
. . . prematurely burned out.''

Let us try to reflect together on why, in our fatherland,
work is generally not a factor that enriches and ennobles
man.

For what reasons is a country that once upon a time
knew how to help other nations today bogged down in
debt and pleading for financial assistance?

Why is man often only a robot charged with accom-
plishing, preferably in silence, a plan decided upon by
theoreticians?

I think that each of those who are present here would
be able to give a goodly number of reasons. Let us examine
some of them.

(1)   *The absence of God*

For decades, systematically, at any price, and on the
official level, there has been a desire to exclude God from
social and economic development. The absence of God
signifies the absence of divine laws, the absence of divine
commandments, and the absence of Christian morality
deeply rooted and sorely tested in the course of the one
thousand-year history of our nation.

God, prayer, and work, united together, help man to
see the meaning of his life and of his struggle. The man
who is working hard without God, without prayer,
without an ideal, will be like a bird with one wing staying close to the ground. It wouldn't know how to raise itself and see the loftiest of possibilities, the highest
meaning of earthly existence. It will turn around on its

beak like a wounded bird. The lamented primate of the millenium, dead these two years, perfectly understood this when he declared, "Open the doors of the factories, of the workshops, hospitals, and of every place of work—from the pinnacle of the sky walks of the factories, down to the deepest depths of the pits of the mines—in order to allow new life to enter . . ."—in order to allow God to enter. In the time of Solidarity, we have seen how it is essential that we not break with God in seeking social and economic transformation.

(2)   *The absence of justice and of truth* (consequently injustice and the lie)

When workers, in order to maintain a family of several persons, are forced to take several jobs or to work on Sundays, we are in the process of murdering the human conscience. We destroy families. We steal from children the time that their parents should be devoting to them. Honest work deserves an honest salary, a just salary. In order to earn more, a miner will have to work on Sunday—at the price of holy Mass, at the price of time that he owes to his family, at the price of his own rest. Without rest, will he work well on Monday? And this miner, receiving for Sunday work at least a double salary, has to ask himself the following question: "Sunday I didn't extract more coal than Friday, perhaps even less, but I have been paid more. When, therefore, did I fool myself, Friday or Sunday?"

Who is responsible for the professional degradation in our fatherland when it is announced that a person is working well and that success follows success, while the worker knows very well that in reality he is doing the exact opposite?

Effort and work demand good internal order, sound moral principles, and even religious motivations if they are to serve man properly. The economy has need of assistance from moral forces.

The employer must allow himself to be guided by

justice. One does not have the right to deprive a man of work or to hinder his professional advancement merely because be professes different opinions, merely because he feels remorse for the conscience of another, merely because his political and moral attitude differs from that which is imposed, merely because he has campaigned actively for Solidarity. All of this does not help us to extricate ourselves from the economic crisis. I even dare to say that such machinations impel us deeper into it.

(3)   *The absence of freedom*
I will recall a passage, already cited here last January, from the declaration of our lamented primate, Cardinal Stefan Wyszynski.

> The world of work has known several deceptions and many limitations during these last decades. The workers and all of society have experienced in Poland great suffering because of the limitation of rights essential to the human person— curtailment of freedom in the area of thought, of outlook on the world, of religious faith, of education for youth. All of that was snuffed out. In the area of professional work, there was created a model of man forced to work and be silent . . .

The personal character of work has therefore been lost. When Solidarity was born in the sorrow and torment of the workers, it was nothing else than a loud cry on the part of the workers for justice—for a greater consciousness of working with us and for us—a major appeal for respect of the worker. Then there was in our fatherland a meaningful process for awakening the conscience and the will to be responsible for the nation, its duty and its social life, and even for the good image of the regime, which must be one of service and not of repression.

(4)   *The absence of respect for human dignity*
There can be no well-being in a country in which man

can be manipulated, in which he can be falsely accused under the pretext of respecting the law, or in which decrees do not have as their purpose the common good of man but instead are often directed against man and designed to cause him suffering. Our bishops have already addressed a number of memoranda to the government on the subject of the decrees that run counter to human values. But even in antiquity Tacitus stated, "The sicker a state is the more it increases its decrees and regulations." Perhaps it is necessary to look also to society for the cause of this illness.

(5) *The absence of love*

Wherever there is injustice, wherever there is repression, lies, hatred, and lack of respect for human dignity, the heart, openness, and self-denial are found to be lacking. Let us not forget that without these values it is difficult to give work its true meaning; it is difficult to lift the country out of crisis. But love must go hand in hand with courage.

Allow me to read here an excerpt from the book of our lamented primate, *The Sacralization of Professional Work*, previously cited on several occasions:

> The Christian only fulfills his professional, familial, national, and state duties by showing himself courageous, by professing his principles, without fear, without shame, without abandoning them through fear and for bread. Woe to that society whose citizens do not conduct themselves with courage! They cease then to be citizens and become instead simple slaves! It is courage which transforms people into citizens—for the courageous man is conscious of his rights and the duties which are incumbent upon him as a member of society. Man is a citizen when he defends his rights in society, when basing himself upon them, he fulfills his professional duties,

his familial, civic, and religious duties. If the
citizen renounces the virtue of courage, he becomes a slave, he does violence to himself by
himself, he does violence to his human personality, to his family, to his professional group, to his
nation, to the state, and to the church, even if he
is manipulated by fear and by fright, for bread
and for other advantages. Woe to rulers who wish
to conquer the citizen at the price of fear and of
groveling like a slave. No longer then are they
men whom they are governing, but, excuse the
word, chattel. If the regime governs citizens because they are overcome by fear, then the regime
degrades its authority. It impoverishes the national cultural life and the value of professional
life. Courage is one of the elements essential to
the life of citizens.

This is why a Christian, the more he has the
duty of love, has the duty of courage.

Let us therefore be strong; let us give proof of courage
and of love; let us live in hope. Let us be certain that
whatever came to pass once upon a time is capable of being removed from the nation. Let us be certain that the
events of the 1980s linked to the word *Solidarity* have, as
the Holy Father said last May 3:

…a great power in the life of the nation, in its
aspirations for identity, in its desire to fashion
the future. Even though we have to bear the burden and the trial of centuries, let us lose neither
certitude nor assurance that these events and
what they signify contribute, as once the May 3
Constitution did, to shaping the life of the nation.
For they come forth from its spirit, they correspond to its spirit, and if it must live, the nation will live by its spirit.

It can, as often happens in history, seem to us today

that we have lost, that we have undertaken a battle doomed to failure, that we have taken a useless risk. However, it is important for us to believe that times are coming in which our efforts and our pains—today unfruitful—will bear their fruit for the good of our beloved fatherland. Amen.

Prayer of the Faithful

Let us pray . . .

—for the Church of Christ, that it be a sign that shows forth to men the way of truth, goodness, love, justice, and peace;

—for our Holy Father, John Paul II, that his pilgrimage in the fatherland strengthen the solidarity of hearts in the struggle against all manifestations of evil;

—for our fatherland, that it may become more and the kingdom of Christ;

—for those who are arrested, condemned, for those who live in hiding and those who have been dismissed from their jobs, for these and for their families, that they find in their sufferings the caring hand of their brothers;

—for the steelworkers of Warsaw, that they witness by their lives, by their fidelity to the motto they have placed on their flag: God, Honor, Fatherland, Faith, and Solidarity;

—for our brothers who have given their lives for liberty and justice in the fatherland on all fronts, in the gulags, the camps, the ghettos, in the course of all the national insurrections, and particularly for the workers of Posnanie, of Gdansk, of Silesia, that their martyred blood serve as a moral renewal for our nation;

—for all those who have put themselves at the service of the lie, injustice, and repression, help them, Lord, to render an account of the shame of their self-humiliation;

—for those who are governing, that they understand that to govern truly means to serve in a spirit of love and justice;

—for our pastor and for Father Jerzy, that God give them strength and steadfastness to accomplish their pastoral mission;

—for ourselves, that we serve truth and justice, despite all the difficulties in our environment, in order to hasten the coming of the final victory of Solidarity.

Hear us, O Lord.

Declaration of a Representative of the Steelworkers

Dear Father Jerzy Popieluszko, chaplain of the steelworkers of Warsaw! Permit me, on the occasion of your birthday and of the second anniversary of the blessing of the flag of Solidarity, which belongs to the steel mills of Warsaw, to address to you some words of gratitude and deep love—having in mind especially your work with us and for us. In this work, by your heroic example, you give proof that the loyal and devoted activity of a pastor, accomplished in union with the people of God, is victorious over evil, over repression and tyranny, and serves to advance the just rights of the workers. You, who were first to stand up before the improvised altar in the victorious days of August, did not abandon us in the dark night of December. You lifted up your voice to speak the truth regarding our union Solidarity, about the need for the rights of workers to be defended in order to lead a life of dignity and to press for moral renewal and self-determination. You spoke about our right to express ourselves regarding our problems with our own voices; your voice is our voice, a cry of protest lifted up before injustice and the big lie. You have constructed the Arch of Solidarity in our hearts in order to have us enter there, we and our families; you have given us words of love and of faith in Christ, on whom we base our hope for common victory. We thank you, Father Jerzy, for all that you have accomplished for us and we address ourselves, by our prayer, to the risen Jesus Christ in order that he preserve

you with good health and that he give you the strength
to accomplish your pastoral ministry for the greater good
of the Christian Polish nation.

Before the Blessing
   I thank you all for your prayer and for your customary
respectful attitude. I recall the recommendations made by
the pastor before this holy mass: let us comport ourselves
with dignity in leaving church and not let ourselves be
disturbed by those whose intentions are different from our
own. Our intention is to comfort one another in love of
the fatherland and to pray for its intentions. Let us say,
as we did last month, that only troublemakers who do not
seek the good of the fatherland are standing in front of the
church. We will see who they are if they show themselves!
And if it should happen that they are not there, we will
all be very happy for that.
   I wish to thank you for having participated in this
common prayer, especially to thank my brother steelworkers who have come to this holy mass not only from the
steel mills of Warsaw, but also from the Lenin steel mills,
the Kosciuszko steel mills, the Hutman steel mills, the
Hutmasz steel mills, and other steelworks throughout the
entire country.
   Receive the blessing of God!

MAY 1983

Before Holy Mass
Therefore, under the vault of the Church,
in which God opens His arms to us,
we turn our faces toward Him
in which He reads our suffering.
There, at the foot of the altar,
at which the priest opens his arms for us,
we offer our hearts
in order that they may be open to God.
And the crowd hears the prayer,
for us who are deceived, beaten down;
for we who are humiliated, imprisoned, exiled;
for us who seek the truth,
and are thirsty for liberty;
for the murdered.
Such a jewel of love,
the prayer wafts toward heaven
for Pope John Paul II,
for him and for our enslaved Fatherland,
for priests who brighten up the darkness of the night,
for Solidarity in chains.
There, at the foot of the altar,
in which the priest opens his arms,
our plea and our desire are poured forth,
our hope and our faith,
and the tears which flow from our eyes.
And under the vault of the Church
God opens to them His heart.
(Teresa, ''Where the Priest Opens His Arms'')

Introduction to the Liturgy
The month of May is especially devoted to the all-holy

Virgin Mother of God. Between the hands of the Mother of God we place our intentions this day, we pray her to carry them before the throne of God the most high:

—our fatherland with its unceasing upsets and uncertainty regarding tomorrow;

—mothers anxious about the threat that hangs over the destiny of their children;

—ill-treated youth, who become the principal goal of the sword of hatred;

—the lamented Gregory Przemyk, whose tragic death symbolizes the sufferings of Polish youth;

—Barbara, his mother, sorrowfully tried, but who bears her cross with dignity;

—those who are deprived of freedom and of work;

—the pilgrimage of the Holy Father in the fatherland, that it contribute to the unification of hearts and of minds comforted by faith, hope, and love;

—everything that causes evil for us and everything that makes us glad, bear it, Mother, before the throne of God the most high.

Reading Apocalypse 12:7–12

And now war broke out in heaven, when Michael with his angels attacked the dragon. The dragon fought back with his angels, but they were defeated and driven out of heaven. The great dragon, the primeval serpent, known as the devil or Satan, who had deceived all the world, was hurled down to the earth and his angels were hurled down with him. Then I heard a voice shout from heaven, 'Victory and power and empire for ever have been won by our God, and all authority for his Christ, now that the persecutor, who accused our brothers day and night before our God, has been brought down. They have tirumphed over him by the blood of the Lamb and by the witness of their martyrdom, because even in the face of death they would not cling to life. Let the heavens rejoice

and all who live there; but for you, earth and sea, trouble
is coming—because the devil has gone down to you in a
rage, knowing that his days are numbered.

Meditation Song: Psalm 64
God, hear me as I make my plea,
protect me from this frightening enemy,
hide me from the wicked and their schemes,
from this mob of evil men,
sharpening their tongues like swords,
shooting bitter words like arrows,
shooting at the innocent from cover,
shooting suddenly, without warning.

Urging each other on to their wicked purpose,
they discuss where to hide their snares.
'Who is going to see us?' they say
'Who can probe our secrets?'
Who? He who probes the inmost mind
and the depths of the heart.

God will shoot them with his own arrow,
wound them without warning.
He will destroy them for that tongue of theirs,
and all who see them fall will shake their heads.

Then all will feel afraid,
will tell others what God has done;
they will understand why he has done it.

The virtuous will rejoice in Yahweh,
will make him their refuge;
and upright hearts will be able to boast.

Gospel: John 19:15–17
Near the cross of Jesus stood his mother and his mother's

sister Mary the wife of Clopas, and Mary of Magdala. Seeing his mother and the disciple he loved standing near her,
Jesus said to his mother, 'Woman, this is your son.' Then
to the disciple he said, 'This is your mother.' And from
that moment the disciple made a place for her in his home.

Homily

"The prayer of sorely tried hearts is always fruitful."
We stand today before the altar of Christ the Lord and our
hearts are weighed down with trials and sorrows. In this
month of Mary, in this month of May, our prayer ascends
before the throne of God to the hands of the most holy
Mother of the Lord. In the awkward words of our prayer,
we wish to express that in which our joy and sorrow
consist.

For a long time you have been Queen of Poland,
Mary—for a long time, for centuries. For a long time you
have been our Mother. For a long time, since the words
addressed to St. John by your Son dying on the cross: "Behold your Mother."

Our nation has adopted you as Mother for more than
a thousand years, when the Polish state began to take
shape.

Over the centuries, you have been Mother and Queen.
You have passed through the centuries of a difficult, magnificent, tragic, and sorrowful history of our nation.

You chose the throne of a Queen and the house of a
Mother when, six hundred years ago, you appeared in the
miraculous image of the Black Virgin of Jasna Gora.

You were at Grunwald[1] when our knights advanced
in bloody and victorious combat against the Teutonic
knights; they had your title, Mother of God, on their lips.

You were with the nation when Father Kordeck un-

[1] The battle in 1410 when the Polish-Lithuanian army conquered the Teutonic knights; a celebrated 19th-century painting by Jan Matejko symbolizes this great date in the Polish conscience.

dertook the heroic defense of Jasna Gora at the time when
the Swedes were beaten back. You accomplished that from
below, from Jasna Gora of the victory, so that the patriotic spirit of love toward the fatherland and the spirit of
struggle against the enemy might spread far and wide.

You were with King John III Sobieski who, before going to Vienna to fight the Turks, knelt at your feel at
Czestochowa and prayed for victory.

You were with us especially during the long slavery,
during the period of partition, when in every possible way,
all trace of Poland was obliterated. It was of you that a female poet was thinking when she wrote, ''My son, my little one, listen. So that you may be Polish, so that you may
say your prayers in Polish, She has defended Poland in
the course of centuries when Poland had to yield to occupation.''

You were with the nation in 1920 when everyone took
up arms in order to defend their independence, which was
restored after more than a century by protecting the fatherland in the wake of the invasion of atheistic bolsheviks.
In the unequal struggle you accomplished a miracle,
which is known in history as the ''miracle of the Vistula.''

You were especially with us at the time when the
church in our fatherland was directed by the ''primate of
the millenium,'' Stefan Cardinal Wyszynski, dead these
last two years, and you helped him in his courageous
struggle when faith was being threatened. An attempt was
being made to impose atheism and secularization forcibly, to stamp out idealism from the hearts of youth, and
to exclude God officially from the life of the nation.

You were there and you conquered, you, our Queen.
But you were there also and suffered, you, our Mother.

Today you are for us more a Mother than a Queen.
But today, more than ever, we have need of a Mother, of
a Mother who understands everything, who wipes away
every tear, and who gives consolation for every pain and

keeps us from losing hope.

But our hope is often threatened when we see the prince of evil return in strength upon our Polish soil.

We have need of you, Mother, who wipes away every tear, for many are our tears these last eighteen months since that shameful night of December 1981. Yes, many are our tears and our sufferings.

A year ago, during the month of May, a month which is consecrated to you, we said in this house of God that a new wave of suffering, of sorrow, and of tears, was being unfurled upon our fatherland.

We have, however, the hope, that in spite of everything, a clearer future will rise up upon the horizon.

Yet Satan, whom you crushed with your foot and who thrashed about in the convulsions of agony—oh, may this be his final agony!—inflicts new sufferings upon us through his lackeys.

From the first day, the month of May this year became the period of Satan's reign in Warsaw. He appears in the form of repression, shows of force, hatred, and the unfurling of lies and defamations.[2] Over a period of forty-eight hours it has not been sufficient for him to imprison so many of our brothers and sisters lest their freedom or their righteousness of thought might enable them to upset the atmosphere of May Day.

It was not enough for him to mount water cannons and motorized regiments, poised in readiness to stir up difficulty for no reason whatsoever, on the Plaza of the Castle, stained by the heroic blood of our fathers.

On the evening of May 3, using a band of flunkies, he went so far as to invade the Cloister of the Franciscan Sisters. He wounded people who devote their time and their energy to giving aid to those who are the most injured by martial law, to those who are imprisoned for the

---

[2]   On May 1 and 3, 1983, as in the preceding year, violent demonstrations took place in the principal cities of Poland.

crime of contrary opinion.

But that was not enough for Satan. He attempted to perpetrate a crime of such horror that every citizen of Warsaw became struck with terror. He broke the spinal column of an innocent youth.[3] In true beastly fashion, he deprived a mother of her only son, for it was not enough for him to hound the mother and her boy on several occasions. On May 1, he arrested the mother and her son, who was scheduled to sit for his baccalaureate exams some days later. It was not enough for him to have wounded this woman in the course of the brutal invasion of the cloister that we have just mentioned.

And silence fell upon the capital, a silence of solidarity that has joined thousands of hearts, in sorrow, in sorrow and prayer. A river of tears has flowed, a river that has watered anew the seed of Solidarity, which perhaps for some people had dried up during recent times.

Woe to Cain who poured forth the blood of his brother, the innocent blood of Abel. For the blood of Abel calls to God himself for vindication!

The day after the death of Gregory, a female poet wrote,
     What will you say,
     when we all find ourselves before God;
     on one side
     the long line of Polish mothers,
     And on the other,
     you, the executioners of their sons?
We will be able to end here our prayer filled with sorrow. But allow us, merciful Mother of God, to say once again what we have said so many times.

You suffer when such a great number of our sisters and our brothers find themselves constantly in prison for

---

[3] The young student Gregory Przemyk; in his memory Father Popieluszko had a cross erected in the garden of his church. He reposes today beneath the shadow of his cross.

their and our opinions. You suffer when prisoners have no status and continue to be treated as disturbers of the peace. You suffer when our imprisoned brothers—such as the steelworker Seweryn Jaworski—whom we know and whom we highly esteem for their fidelity to ideals, are beaten and mistreated.

You suffer with the mothers whose children are threatened by those who pretend to guarantee order and security.

You know, Mother, that they must not ill-treat a nation that has suffered so much in the course of centuries, that has won so many victories, that has given so much to European and world culture, that has given and will always give to the world so many magnificent persons— this nation that has just given a pope to the world, a pope who is the marvel of the world. Such a nation will not be brought to its knees by the repression of any satanic force. This nation has shown that it only bends the knee before God. And that is why we are confident that God himself will encourage this nation.

And while we await the arrival of the Holy Father to our fatherland, which is his own, we are confident that through him the Holy Spirit will show Himself, that He will renew the face of our martyred land; and may our prayer, the prayer of hearts that are being sorely tried, the prayer inspired by the Holy Father, be fruitful and effective. Amen.

Prayer of the Faithful

Let us pray . . .

—for our Holy Father John Paul II, that his coming to our fatherland will confirm the nation in the hope of victory of good over evil;

—for our martyred fatherland, that the so greatly desired time of true freedom, justice, and love will come;

—for Gregory Przemyk, murdered in a beastly

fashion, and for all those who have been stricken and ill-treated during the month of May, that innocent blood and suffering contribute to strengthening the solidarity of our hearts in our struggle against repression and the big lie;

—for Barbara, the sorrowing mother of Gregory, that she have enough strength to bear her cross;

—for all mothers, that they raise their children in the spirit of love of God and of the fatherland;

—for those who have been arrested, condemned, those who live in hiding, those who have been fired from their jobs, that they encounter good will and sympathy on the part of their own;

—for those who have placed themselves at the service of the big lie, of injustice and oppression, enlighten their hearts, O Lord, and give them the grace of conversion;

—that the media, through the press, radio and television stations may be able to report the truth and nothing but the truth;

—for those governing, that they remember that only power given by the people is sacred and that they do not inflict sufferings on their own nation;

—for ourselves, that we be liberated from fear, fright, and from every spirit of vengeance;

Hear us, O Lord.

Prayer after Communion
Again
we lift up our hands which bear crosses
under the vault of the Church,
this is our profession of faith.
Enervated by the weight of these days,
we gather together before God,
in our hearts the hope of the Church
for the progress of the Fatherland.
Prayer fills us with emotion.

We are out of breath,
we learn love and courage
which are never too great.
Here we mark our presence
by calling humbly upon God;
pardon us our sins
and do not test us.
May the bird guide us toward heaven,
may he open to us the gates of Time
in which there will be no place
for repression, treason, lying.
We pray you, have pity on us;
for those who are bitter and for those who doubt
for those who are uncertain of their lot,
for all of us, give us Your peace.

(Anonymous)

Before the Blessing

This cross here before you was consecrated in a sub-section of FSO for the headquarters of Solidarity. Today we welcome this cross for which a place is lacking at headquarters. We welcome it into our Church.

I address a request to those who come to the masses out of obedience to their orders. Have a little honesty toward your superiors; instruct them accurately about what you have seen and heard here so that your superiors will not look ridiculous in accusing us of false, trumped up charges of the quality of a cheap detective story.

I most warmly thank all of those who have participated in the funeral rite of the late lamented Gregory Przemyk. Many thanks for your silence of solidarity, which said much more than the shouts and the chanting. You have demonstrated once more that these are not citizens of Warsaw, assembled in such great numbers, who are provoking confrontations on the streets. The source of the disturbance, of the disruptions, is undoubtedly to be looked for elsewhere. I pray you again today to leave the Church with dignity and silence in order to return to your homes—in prayer and recollection. Everything that is not recollection can only proceed from enemies of the fatherland, from troublemakers. We will depart then in profound silence.

JUNE 1983

Introduction to the Liturgy

In this month of the Sacred Heart, month of the grace of God spread over all the people of God, in this historic month of the second pilgrimage of our Holy Father John Paul II to his native land, we gather together to pray for the fatherland, keeping in mind all of its difficult problems.

As always, we carry in our hearts our fatherland, all those who suffer, who are imprisoned for their opinions, who are excluded from their jobs, in hiding, industrial workers and workers in the field, all the various artistic circles, and especially the young, children who are subjected to problems not of their own making and who later will be responsible for the fatherland.

Today we again thank God for the grace that is the pilgrimage of the Holy Father and we pray that the pain of the pilgrim may be extremely fruitful. May we let nothing escape from the vast patrimony of the Word of God which flows from his mouth.

Reading: Wisdom 10:8–16
For, by neglecting the path of Wisdom,
not only were they kept from knowledge of the good,
they actually left the world a memorial of their folly,
so that their crimes might not escape notice.

But Wisdom delivered her servants from their ordeals.
The virtuous man fleeing from the anger of his
brother,
was led by her along straight paths.
She showed him the kingdom of God
and taught him the knowledge of holy things.

She brought his success in his toil
and gave him full return for all his efforts;
she stood by him against grasping and oppressive men
and she made him rich.

She guarded him closely from his enemies
and saved him from the traps they set for him.
In an arduous struggle she awarded him the prize,
to teach him that piety is stronger than all.

She did not foresake the virtuous man when he was
sold,
but kept him free from sin;
she would not abandon him in his chains,
but procured for him the sceptre of a kingdom
and authority over his despotic masters,
thus exposing as liars those who had traduced him,
and giving him honour everlasting.

A holy people and a blameless race,
this she delivered from a nation of oppressors.
She entered the soul of a servant of the Lord,
and withstood fearsome kings with wonders and
signs.

Meditation Song: Psalm 85
Yahweh, you favour your own country,
you bring back the captives of Jacob,
you take your people's guilt away,
you blot out all their sins,
you retract all your anger,
you abjure your fiery rage.

Bring us back, God our saviour,
master your resentment against us.
Do you mean to be angry with us forever,

to prolong your wrath age after age?

Will you not give us life again,
for your people to rejoice in you?
Yahweh, show us your love,
grant us your saving help.

I am listening. What is Yahweh saying?
What God is saying means peace
for his people, for his friends,
if only they renounce their folly;
for those who fear him, his saving help is near,
and the glory will then live in our country.

Love and Loyalty now meet,
Righteousness and Peace now embrace;
Loyalty reaches up from earth
and Righteousness leans down from heaven.

Yahweh himself bestows happiness
as our soil gives its harvest,
Righteousness always preceding him
and Peace following his footsteps.

Gospel: Luke 9:18–23

Now one day when he was praying alone in the
presence of his disciples he put this question to them,
'Who do the crowds say I am?' And they answered, 'John
the Baptist; others Elijah; and others say one of the ancient
prophets come back to life.' 'But you,' he said, 'who do
you say I am?' It was Peter who spoke up. 'The Christ of
God' he said. But he gave them strict orders not to tell anyone anything about this.

'The Son of Man' he said 'is destined to suffer grie-
vously, to be rejected by the elders and chief priests and
scribes and to be put to death, and to be raised up on the

third day.'

Then to all he said, 'If anyone wants to be a follower of mine, let him renounce himself and take up his cross every day and follow me.'

Homily

Despite the black night into which our sorrowful fatherland has been plunged, despite the hopes that wane, despite our sufferings, despite the tragic and sorrowful events of these last nineteen months, despite the humiliation of human dignity, despite the disturbance of parents over the future destiny of their children, despite the worst difficulties, a ray of the grace of God has shown forth upon our fatherland: the visit of our Holy Father John Paul II. He came to announce peace.

When he embraced the soil of his native land, as one kissing the hands of a beloved mother, he pronounced these words:

"Peace be upon you, Poland, my fatherland; Peace be to you!"

And during the entire period of his presence, and with a great deal of personal fatigue, the illustrious pilgrim pointed out the way to peace for our fatherland.

With much dignity, understanding, and courage, he tackled all the problems of our daily life.

Today we do not wish to mention the problems that have complicated the pilgrimage of the Polish pope and our participation in it. We do not wish to speak of the media, especially of television, which, in a very disagreeable fashion, showed, in the manner of its coverage, less than enthusiastic understanding of this great national event—chicanery on the part of weak and misguided spirits. Let us today forget these problems. Looking back, in our prayer and our faith, we wish to render homage to one who is the greatest Pole in the one thousand years of our country's history. We wish to reflect for an instant today on the riches that he has brought to us by means of his pilgrimage and left us for our meditation.

Let us first of all thank Almighty God for having comforted us, those who have been gathering together for a year and a half to pray in this church of Zoliborz for the fatherland, for freedom, for love and justice, for truth, for the strengthening of hope, for liberation of prisoners, for the dignity of human work, for concern for what was acquired in August 1980, for needed dialogue and a social agreement based on honesty, and, as usual, all other intentions.

On arrival at the airport, the Holy Father pronounced significant words regarding Poland, our mother, who has suffered so much and who is suffering once more. Immediately afterward, he declared,

> I beg those who suffer to be especially near me. I beg them, using the words of Christ: "I was sick and you came to me, I was in prison and you came to me (Matthew 25:35). By myself I cannot visit all the sick, prisoners, and the suffering, but I pray them to be near me in spirit that they may help me, as they always do. I have received many letters which bear witness to this, especially in recent times."

Some prisoners from Rakowiecka responded in a special way. They offered up a strict fast with their prayers during the course of the Holy Father's trip to the fatherland. On the occasion of the appeal at Jasna Gora on June 19, the Holy Father prayed in a sorrowful voice: "I pray, O Mother of my nation, for those who suffer and for those who inflict sufferings."

In speaking of freedom in a place where Poles have always felt themselves to be free, at Jasna Gora, he appropriately stated,

> We are children of God, we cannot be slaves. Our divine "sonship" in itself carries the heritage of

freedom. Freedom, given to man by God, as a measure of His greatness . . . A state is really sovereign if it governs society and at the same time serves the common good of society and if it permits the nation to fulfill its nature as a moral person and to secure its own identity.

The Pope was referring to the repeal of several concessions acquired in August 1980. He stressed the necessity of drafting an agreement and entering into dialogue precisely on these matters.

On the occasion of the meeting with the prime minister at Belvedere Palace, the Holy Father said,

Even though life in the fatherland has endured since December 13, 1981, the very difficult trials of martial law, I do not cease hoping that the announced social renewal, based on principles hammered out at the price of important initiatives during the decisive days of August 1980 and contained in the accords, will achieve its ends. This renewal is indispensable for maintaining the good name of Poland in the world, for getting out of the present internal crisis, for sparing sufferings to numerous daughters and numerous sons of the nation, my fellow countrymen.

While speaking at Wroclaw about truth and justice, the Pope said that truth is the basis of confidence and the strength of love. In a spirit of love and not of repression, man is ready to accept the most difficult and the most demanding truth. Confidence in the nation is achieved by truth and by love. The aspiration for justice in the fatherland flows from the healthy wellsprings of the Polish spirit, from deep respect for the dignity of human work, for love of the fatherland, and for solidarity, that is to say, deep respect and high regard for the common good.

In speaking to the workers at Katowice, he said,

The entire world has followed, and continues to

follow, with emotion the events which have taken place in Poland since August 1980. What has especially caused public opinion to pause to reflect is the moral aspect of human work. Salary increases were not number one in these events. Another striking fact: these events were without any violence, no one was killed, no one was wounded. Finally these events, affecting the world of the Polish worker during these years of the eighties, were clearly marked by a religious focus. Social justice consists in a respect for and in a realization of the rights of man in relation to all the members of a society.

The rights of the worker are many. Among the most important permit us to cite

. . . the right to a just wage, that is to say, what is sufficient to maintain a family.

. . . the right of associating freely with members of particular professions.

This right, the Holy Father says, in quoting our lamented primate, is not a concession on the part of anyone—it is an innate right. That is why the state does not have to confer this right. Its role and its duty are to protect it and to be vigilant lest it be infringed upon.

Consequently, the particular type of union that is capable of existing cannot be imposed by the state.

The worker is not only an instrument of production, he is a subject.

Man must be the first priority.

The worker is ready for deprivations if he feels himself at home and if he can have a say about the just and fair distribution of created goods. Man is incapable of working well if he does not perceive the meaning of his work, if this work ceases to be evident to him, if it is in some way hidden.

We are in agreement with the Holy Father's addressing himself to the young, who gathered together in such great numbers at Jasna Gora; we do not want a Poland that counts them for naught.

We can give a great deal of our lives to the fatherland, but we need guarantees that this sacrifice will not be wasted.

We hope that the government may understand that it can only be strong by putting its reliance on society, and the way that leads there does so by means of respect for man, for his conscience and his opinions.

The words of the Holy Father, spoken at Cracow, will resound in our ears for a long time:

You must be strong with the strength of faith,
You must be strong with the strength of hope.
You must be strong with the strength of love,
with love which supports everything.
The nation, insofar as it is a human community, is called to victory, to victory by the force of faith, of hope, of love, by the force of truth, of freedom, and of justice.

These are only some of the Holy Father's thoughts that can help us on the road to a better future in the fatherland—a road that he pointed out to us on the occasion of his pilgrimage. We will reflect in detail upon his directives at our monthly masses for the fatherland.

It merely depends upon us to know how we are going to take to the road that he has shown to us. To the extent that we find our proper place on that road, to that extent will we courageously drive out evil wherever God places us for the rest of our days. To that end let us place in our hearts the words of the psalm that the Holy father repeated several times at Cracow: "The Lord is my shepherd . . . Even if I march through the valley of darkness, I fear no evil because You are with me."

We will not fear any evil for we know today that he, John Paul II, the vicar of Christ, is with us with all his heart, with all his strength. We will not fear evil for the Lord himself is with us. Amen.

Prayer of the Faithful

Let us pray . . .

—for the Church of Christ, that she enfold in her love all the suffering, those who are suffering for justice and freedom;

—for Pope John Paul II, that the Divine Word that he has spoken on our Polish soil bear abundant fruit for the Church and for the fatherland in the near future;

—that we do not allow ourselves to dissipate the very rich heritage that has been left to us at the price of great personal fatigue on the part of the Holy Father;

—for our fatherland, that it increases in justice, freedom, and love for the good of the entire world;

—for the media, that they seek to transmit throughout our fatherland only the truth, and nothing but the truth;

—for the liberation of prisoners, the employment of those dismissed from their jobs, the readmittance to schools of our brothers who are opposed to injustice;

—for those who govern us, that they may be inspired by the spirit of love and justice and not by that of repression;

—that the suffering, tears, and innocent blood poured out contribute to increased solidarity of hearts in our fatherland;

—that we preserve, free from repression, the ideals for which we have struggled in the ranks of Solidarity;

—for the strengthening of faith, hope, and love in our hearts.

—Hear us, O Lord.

Before the Blessing

Our presence and numbers here are a sufficient demonstration of our patriotic sentiments. Do not lose this spirit that vivifies us; let us not make it easy work for those who seek to disturb our atmosphere of prayer and love for the fatherland.

190 The Way of My Cross

JULY 1983*

Introduction to the Liturgy

As on every last Sunday of the month, we come to-day to the house of the Lord to pray for our fatherland.

What are we going to bring today, the last day of July of the year 1983?—always, gratitude to the Holy Father for the words of comfort and of hope that he brought to us last month. These words will ever sound in our heads and should stir our hearts and minds to action.

On the eve of the thirty-ninth anniversary of the Warsaw uprising, we bring the remembrance of the insurgents' heroism our gratitude but also deep regret for the many victims—due, first of all, to the fact that Warsaw had been abandoned by its allies. Instead of coming to help it, they looked on as it lay in a bloody agony.

In the lifting of the state of seige, which the Bishops have demanded so many times, we regret that once more the initiative has not been taken to bring the nation together. We have considered the amnesty a strategy. However, the nation was right to expect that amnesty might cause all the contraventions to martial law to be for-gotten and that the hardships, especially moral hardship, might be compensated for. But our brothers, democrati-cally elected and highly esteemed by the majority of Poles, are being kept in prison while those, benefiting from am-nesty, feel that they are hostages.

We regret that the nation is shackled by so many new regulations that it seems as if the chains, partially removed from its hands, are being placed instead on souls and con-sciences.

Thus, everything that we have experienced in the

* Father Popieluszko was not present in July at St. Stanislas Church.

month of July, including our enduring love of the Fatherland, we unite in the offering of Christ, and we pray him to reinforce our faith, our hope, and our love.

Before the Blessing

I thank you all very warmly for your common prayer for the intentions of the fatherland; I thank very particularly our sisters and our brothers who come to this house of God from very distant districts of our country. I therefore thank the representatives of Torun, of Gdansk, of Kolorzeg, of Slupski, of Bytom, of Piekary, of Gliwice, of Tarnowskie Gory, of Szczecin, and of Lublin, whom I know to be among us, as well as all of those towns I have not mentioned.

At the same time, I invite you to a holy mass for the fatherland in a month, August 20, as usual at 7:00 in the evening. This mass will have a special character because it will be the third anniversary of the workers' struggles in August, from which Solidarity was born. For the workers of the Warsaw steel mills it commemorates the day on which they began the Solidarity strike in order to support the workers of Gdansk. The steelworkers must not forget that Sweryn Jaworski, whom they then elected president of their strike committee, is, to this very day, still in prison.

AUGUST 1983

Homily

Today, on this third anniversary of one of the attempts at our country's rebirth, it would be enough to gather ourselves together to recall in our memories those warm days of August 1980 when the Polish nation's Solidarity was born. In sorrow, weariness of heart, uncertainty about tomorrow, and much spiritual and physical effort, Solidarity was born out of concern for the land of our birth. We were on our knees before improvised altars with the rosary in hand and some patriotic and religious songs on our lips. Solidarity was born in a patriotic outburst of workers assisted by intellectuals and artists. Solidarity simply branched out and became stronger, like a mighty tree. Today her branches are shorn, her crown cut, but her roots remain deep and solid because they plunge down into the hearts and minds of man. This is why Solidarity will continue to expand: she will recall to the world that she *is*, that she *exists*, that she *lives*.

I would hope that our getting together today will bear fruit beyond the house of God in meetings between friends and fellow workers. May there be now added to the long thread of our years whatever is good, beautiful, and noble in our Fatherland, and may this permeate more and more deeply into our daily lives!

We are going to reflect today, on this anniversary, by beginning with words laden with meaning: Freedom, Truth, Justice, and Solidarity.

FREEDOM. The earthly activity of Christ aimed for understanding of this very important reality: we have been created for freedom, for the freedom of the children of God. God created man free to the extent that he can accept God or reject Him. Freedom is a value that God inscribed in man at his creation. Lack of respect for the right to freedom—above all, that of conscience and of integrity—is an action against the Creator himself.

In our fatherland, after the period of curtailment of individual freedom, the nation was, by right, expecting that the state of siege would be ended by the regime, that the amnesty would allow suspicions and recriminations to be forgotten, and that the status of a moral person would be recognized for society—as the Holy Father had many times requested—thereby making possible the resumption of dialogue (interrupted in December 1981) between the regime and the nation. The nation was totally correct in waiting for the first step toward a mutual and peaceful restoration of the fatherland.

TRUTH. Truth resides in the agreement of words and acts. Truth cannot tolerate beautiful words and declarations about an agreement if, at the same time, citizens are being deprived of their rights. But the recent rules adopted by Parliment certainly do not square with the correct meaning of the common good and best interest of society. They further whittle away the severely curtailed freedoms of citizens, freedoms that existed not only before 1980 but even before 1956. They make a mockery of freedom of thought and independence in the operation of high schools. They are aimed at freedom of opinion for young students.

Has nothing changed since the time of Plato, who stated "Every government enacts laws for its own interest?"

Then how are we to appreciate a regime that seeks to recover its authority by means of regulations and decrees?

Truth resides in the agreement of words and actions.

It is true that, for God, man is king of creation: he must not be subjected to ends contrary to his final destiny, which is eternal life with God.

As Lech Walesa correctly said in the course of his conversation with the Holy Father on June 27, the August somersault has caused a profound transformation. The nation knows what it wants, and this interior transformation is irreversible.

Indeed, the solidarity of the nation has increased at the price of tears, sufferings, and the blood of workers, and it was born out of concern for the fatherland. It is also true that the August agreements have been signed with Solidarity, therefore with the national movement and not simply with a union created some months later. Consequently, the breaking of the August agreements in such a brutal fashion, during the night in December 1981, was the rupturing of a dialogue with the nation. For, as the bishops stated on December 15, two days after the inauguration of the state of war: "The decision of the authorities wields a blow to the expectation of society and the hope of seeing the problems of our fatherland resolved by negotiations."

Certainly Solidarity has the right to exist freely since it has paid the price to do so. This has cost the nation dearly. Some have had to pay for it with the supreme price of their lives. There are many others who have paid for it by the loss of their liberty over the course of many months; many are those who have had to leave their country. Those who have been the most faithful to their opinions and to their conscience find themselves imprisoned. Many are those who have been forced to sign declarations contrary to their convictions. The primate of Poland spoke of this on January 6, 1982: "It is more and more common to demand workers to sign all sorts of declarations, especially declarations about leaving Solidarity which, should they refuse, results in their being dismissed from their place of work."

It is therefore the right to exist that has been paid for by so many physical and moral sufferings.

It is true that the nation, reduced for decades to silent productivity, has sometimes "anteed up" and exceed-

ed its bounds. But it is also true, as the deceased primate
of Poland declared two years ago, that Solidarity has accomplished more in a few months than the most effective
political system could have done.

It is true that in the space of a very short time millions
of people spontaneously came together and, on their own
initiative, joined Solidarity. As for the present situation
of new unions, you who have been subjected to all sorts
of pressures know much better than anyone else.

JUSTICE. Justice signifies equality before the law and
independence of the courts. It implies the possibility of
responding by way of the press, without risking the em-
bargo of censure, for a defamatory article such as the one
against the church that appeared in the weekly *Life of the
Party*, dated August 17, 1983. And it is important, I believe, to add here the words of the late lamented Cardinal Stefan Wyszynski: ''When an enemy struggles against
the church, this serves him well in his struggle against the
nation.''

Justice recognizes the rights of each person. It is a just
salary for an honest day's work. It is forbidden to dismiss
or denigrate a man merely because he works differently
for the welfare of the fatherland.

Justice makes possible the response to the reproaches
aimed at Solidarity, for example, in the pamphlet entitled
The Agreements of August, which one can buy—today
when publications are so expensive—for the modest sum
of eighteen zlotys. It allows the defamatory accusations
publicly launched by the media to become a source of em-
barassment, as was the case during recent weeks with
respect to Lech Walesa. Justice is the pluralism of which
we were assured even during martial law: the pluralism
of unions, of artistic circles, without the exclusive protection of but one patron. It is the creation of favorable conditions for the formation of young people's personalities
according to principles freely chosen and not imposed,

permitting them to learn about life through youth organizations whose guiding principles square with their own, as the Polish Bishops have affirmed in the past.

Justice is amnesty, it is both total repeal of punishments for activities contrary to the decree of martial law and compensation for moral injuries. It is a social compact guaranteeing the nation that it will not be betrayed once more and that in a few years the climate for the mutual construction of the new society will not prove to be one of errors and deviations. May the pain and the effort of the nation not have been totally in vain!

SOLIDARITY. Solidarity is the unity of hearts, of minds and of hands, rooted in ideals capable of transforming the world. It is the hope of millions of Poles, the hope that becomes much stronger as it flows from the source of all hope, namely God.

Solidarity, as the Holy Father remarked during his return from Africa, is the unity of the community. It is the guiding principle and basic orientation given to the Poles during the 1980s. It is a lively appeal to respect for human dignity; it is, at the same time, concern for each person and his or her problems. It is concern for those who are imprisoned, a demand for their liberation for assistance and protection to be accorded their families.

It is brotherly concern for all those who have been bullied and hassled for their opinions, for our opinions. It is important for us to explain to young people the many historic problems of our fatherland.

Solidarity, finally, is love for one's native land; it is the maintenance of inner freedom even when conditions of slavery exist outside. It is the defense of the dignity of the child of God and the courageous recognition of ideals that we are defending and that we carry in our hearts.

We will end these reflections today with the words pronounced by the Holy Father when he was still Archbishop of Cracow, words that I previously quoted last October: "Weak are a people if they accept their own defeat, it they forget that they have been sent to watch until their hour comes; for the hours ceaselessly return on the great sundial of history."

Nevertheless, let us remember that strong are a people who establish their life and their fatherland on Truth, Love, Justice, and Solidarity of hearts and minds, in a union of prayer with the source of these values, the Father of peoples and of nations, the Eternal God.

Amen.

SEPTEMBER 1983

Homily

Sent to the entire world to bear the Good News to all peoples and to all nations, Jesus Christ nevertheless had his own native land—a native land with its tradition, its history, its religion, and its culture. He submitted himself to the just laws of his fatherland even though none, insofar as he was God, applied to him. Christ wanted thereby to stress how highly important it is for each man to possess his own fatherland. Every man is bound to a fatherland by his family, by his place of birth. The fatherland is the local community of his culture, his past, his joyful or sorrowful history. It is the richness of language, of works of art and of music; it is his religion and his customs.

In the course of today's reflections, I would like us to dwell upon the word *culture*. I am perfectly cognizant of the fact that it is a rather fluid subject; for ten minutes, I merely want to point out or raise several questions regarding the concept.

The Holy Father, Pope John Paul II, in addressing youth during his first pilgrimage to his fatherland, declared, "Culture is the expression of man. It is a confirmation of the human condition. Man creates culture and is created through culture . . . Culture is the common good of the nation."

Polish culture is a possession on which the spiritual welfare of Poles is based. Throughout the long history of our fatherland Polish culture has formed and determined us even more than material forces or political frontiers. Thanks to culture, the nation remains herself, despite the loss of her independence for several years. Spiritually, the nation has always been independent because she possesses her own magnificent culture. From the beginning Polish culture bore the evident mark of Christianity. Christianity has always found an echo in the history of thought and artistic creation, in poetry, music, theatre, painting, and sculpture. For centuries Polish culture has drawn its inspiration from the gospel. Adam Mickiewicz, our great national poet, wrote that a civilization truly worthy of man must be Christian. By Christianity, we are bound to western culture and that is why we have been able in the past to reject all the various cultures of barbaric peoples. We have been able to resist cultures that our enemies have imposed upon us.

After the war it was decided that God and the gospel would no longer have their place in the life of the nation and especially that the younger generation would be raised without God.

But we forgot that God was not obliged to submit himself to some of these decrees.

Today we courageously need to reclaim for the nation the right to serve, the right to love, the right to freedom of conscience, to culture, and to our national heritage. We cannot create a history without a past; we cannot forget the Christian orientation of our Nation. Otherwise we gouge out the roots of our more than one-thousand-year past, because a tree without roots withers: we have had many examples of this in the course of recent decades.

We cannot take the nation back to its origins. It is important for us to speak up when culture, literature, and national art are relegated to the last place in school education; when Christian morality, already seriously downplayed, is replaced by a supposed socialist morality, and when teachers in the schools of Warsaw inform Christian parents that children will be brought up with a secular mindset. To deprive children of Christian truth, which was properly prized in Poland for centuries, is to separate them from Poland. It is quite simply, a work of "depolandization." The school must lead children and young people to love of the fatherland, respect for Polish culture. It cannot be a supranational institution that interests itself solely in the present. It must join the past of the fatherland to its future. And since the school is not fulfilling this mission, Christian parents are faced with an even heavier duty. The culture of the nation is also its morality. A Christian nation must be guided in accordance with Christian morality, tried and proven over a period of centuries. A Christian nation has no need of an alleged secular morality, for it is faceless and without hope, as the late lamented primate of the millenium stated. This constitutes a threat to the spiritual values of the nation and it weakens the forces that determine the unity of the nation.

The nation is not to be left to fall apart, despite partitions and insurrections—despite Siberia, "depolandization," Russification, and Kulturkampf— since it is so profoundly rooted in past Polish history. It is not letting itself self-destruct, for it is nourished by history and the culture of past centuries.

From what source should the nation be nourishing itself in the near future with respect to history and present-day culture? Would it be able to be nourished by the lying articles in Rzeczpospolita, Trybuna Ludu, or Argumenty? Is not the soul of youth being deprived of national culture and of the magnificent national history marked every moment along the way by Christianity? Historical facts are rubbed out, passed over in silence. Would it be nourished by attacks against Solidarity and false accusations launched against its directors who were democratically elected by the nation? Is it going to be nourished by banning crucifixes from schools and from factories, a matter which is especially upsetting to the Polish bishops?

Actions against the national culture of a Christian country and a style of government contrary to Christian traditions and personal and family rights, are both measures that do not favor the flourishing of culture.

Only a nation spiritually free and committed to truth can endure and create for the future as the rebels who died on battlefields have done or as the visionary poets have done—poets such as Slowacki, living in exile, who was able to look into the future of Poland, at that time erased from the map, to see a Pole sitting on the throne of Peter.

Only a nation healthy in spirit and conscience can courageously create its future. Let us also cultivate independence of spirit; let us not allow ourselves to be invaded by fear and dread. Let us not imprison the spirit of the nation, even in the most insignificant things. Zygmunt Krasinski warned us about this when he wrote "Siberia is nothing, the yoke nothing, only the poisoned spirit of the nation causes the sorrow of the sorrowful."

Much earlier, Pawel Wlodkowic, said that cultural possessions and spiritual forces will not be conquered by iron and the sword, by force, repression, and violence, but by freedom, love, and respect for rights[1]. An open heart, not closed fists, conquer people. True wisdom, true knowledge, and true culture cannot be enchained. It is not possible to chain human minds. That is why we consider it a totally absurd situation when we see, for example, the administration of a high school "stepping on" an eminent professor of worldwide reputation.

It is worse still, according to the words of Cardinal Stefan Wyszynski, when the state hires "its own" people in order to ensure that men of science think properly that is to say, not in accordance with truth but with politics. All attempts at alienation of the human mind, which itself must create culture, result in the opposite of culture.

On the occasion of the patriotic leap forward by workers in August 1980, the creators of culture were involved in large numbers—actors, journalists, writers,

[1] Pawel Wlodkowic (ca. 1370-1435) was philosopher jurist, and Polish diplomat; he participated in the Council of Constance.

202 The Way of My Cross

artists. Their consciences were raised along with the conscience of the entire nation, which had been anesthetized during these recent decades. The year 1980 became difficult, but it unleashed tremendous qualities that lay dormant in the nation: perspicacity, prudence, and capacity for common activity.

The social, professional, economic, cultural, and political conscience was awakened. Artists set about speaking in an authentic fashion. They decided to serve truth, to serve it through their talent and their craft, to serve truth in the fatherland, this same Polish fatherland that their ancestors unhesitatingly served.

But wherever the Big Lie is, so to speak, cultivated officially, there is no place for truth that unmasks and runs so totally contrary to it. Thus the struggle has once again been taken up against truth, freedom of speech, liberty, and the pluralism of opinions expressed openly and dictated by an enlightened conscience. Some, therefore, have undertaken to consider every demonstration expressing respect for the rights of man a hostile activity. But, back in 1978 in a letter to Kakol, the minister of worship, the primate of the millenium declared;

> The defense of rights is no longer a political
> activity, it is simply the duty of the citizen; it
> is among those who have the cowardice of
> remaining silent that it is fitting to look for the
> enemies of the socialist state, and not among
> those who wish to know the truth about Poland,
> deformed by the official party line.

Conscience, once awakened, will easily distinguish truth from falsehood, good grain from the tares. It understands easily that some important words of command, issued with the mighty reenforcement of waving flags, are empty if, at the same time, there remain in prison brothers whose consciences are clear, brothers who concerned themselves with the welfare of the fatherland—as was the case with Sewery Jaworski, the steelworker of Warsaw. If new arrests continue to be made, an atmosphere of guardedness and surveillance will thereby be created.

In recent times, those in artistic circles have set a great example for us, especially the actors who, since December 13, have demonstrated courage, strength of character, and a spirit of sacrifice exceptional in the history of Poland since the war.

Today the church is preoccupied with new threats that affect the development of Polish culture. The bishops have on several occasions, especially in February 1982 expressed in writing that religion and culture have a basic importance in the maintenance of the social compact. For example, it is indispensable to guarantee the total independence of religious life and the development of culture. The editing of Catholic publications according to the needs of believers and the guarantee of pluralism in cultural undertakings will be a concrete manifestation of this. Last February the bishops followed with great interest the problems that threatened those responsible for culture and art and whose participation in the life of the country is indispensable. Men of culture and art must have conditions of life that guarantee their ability to work and to organize themselves into associations. It is incomprehensible and prejudicial to decide to disband associations of artists, actors, journalists, and, quite recently, the Union of Men of Letters, which has existed without interruption for sixty years—that is to say, since the time of Stefan Zeromski, who founded this association. These decisions are all the more incomprehensible and prejudicial because the statutes of these associations have been approved by these same authorities: yet not one of them has changed a statute during martial law. How do we interpret the declaration, recalled a year ago by the bishops, by which the Military Council of National

Safety—at the time of its proclamation of martial law—
let it be known that these associations could resume their
activities in accordance with their respective statutes?

The development of culture is not favored any longer
by the censorship which in a special way silences the real
Catholic journals—and not the pseudo-Catholic ones—
by striking out words, phrases, entire articles, and true-
to-life, courageous reflections. It strikes out what some
pens, dipped into the ink of truth have written, for these
words could not be true unless they were based on real life.

Lying words are thrown on the trash heap the day
after their publication, even if they were printed in
millions of copies. Catholic reviews and periodicals
riddled with censorship will be a very poor basis for future
history.

Finally, culture is an honest dialogue and an
exchange of opinions—an honest verbal combat, not the
quarrelsome and polemical mindset of professionals who
cast slurs on people through the media without allowing
these people to respond to them. For three weeks, the
primate made clear reference to this.

Let us terminate today's reflection with a prayer from
the Holy Father who said, in addressing the Mother of God
March 31, 1982: "To you, Mother of Jasna Gora, we
confide, most especially, Polish culture now and in the
future. May the life of the nation be maintained and
developed."

Amen.

OCTOBER 1983

Homily

Most Holy Father, we would like to express by this letter, our warmest gratitude for your goodness, your wisdom, your faith, your hope, and your love, which knows no bounds. You are the finest son of our nation.

We want to offer to you what unites us together each month in this house of God.

We wish to offer to you our love for God and for the fatherland.

We wish to thank you for having, from the first day of your pontificate, summoned the world to open wide the gates to Christ.

We thank you for the breath of the Holy Spirit upon your native land, which was manifested on the occasion of your first pilgrimage through your prayer and the words which you spoke at Warsaw and which we all remember: "May your Spirit descend, and renew the face of the earth, of this earth." We thank you for your confirmation of history and of the nation's spiritual setbacks that precede moral renewal. We thank you for this renewal, which will last in spite of the various trials experienced up till now.

During this period of alienation, you have been and you are, the one who confirms us in the hope of victory—of good over evil, love over hatred, truth over the lie.

The most marvelous expression of your concern for the problems of the fatherland has been the great prayer regarding martial law addressed to the Queen of Poland, our Lady of Jasna Gora.

You have preoccupied yourself with all of us. You responded to the letters of prisoners who wrote to you to be with them as they were with you. You have formulated your response in a prayer: "Be with them, 0 Mother, be with those who are condemmed, without trial, to the loss of their freedom, be with all those who suffer on account of the imprisonment of their relatives and their loved ones.''

When it was proposed to our brothers that they leave the fatherland in exchange for their freedom, you cried out with sorrow: ''There is no need for a place to be lacking in Poland for Poles; every man has a right to his fatherland. No one can be condemned to exile.'' We are grateful to you for having employed this word *Solidarity* that is so dear, for having always pointed it out on the banners. It is you, Holy Father, who said with emotion on your return from Africa that you would never forget the main square at Kaduna in Nigeria where, among hundreds of thousands of persons, there was a group of Poles: above them floated a white-and-red flag with the inscription *Solidarity*. And you explained on this occasion that *Solidarity* is not only an expression of anxiety and upset but also the name for communion and unity, an objective which Poles have determined for the eighties.

No other person but you, 0 Holy Father, could point out evil and its machinations with so much force; none other than yourself was able to sense the problems of the fatherland with such great intensity!

Often your prayer overflows with suffering: ''From the thirteenth of December,'' you said, while weeping on the anniversary of the attempt to assassinate you, ''I was suffering with my nation.'' And on the same day, you recalled that the state cannot exercise its power except by having recourse to force.

We thank you for being so interested in each event that has taken place in the fatherland. You think with great concern of those in prison who have gone as far as initiating a hunger strike. We are, above all, thankful to you, Holy Father, for your second pilgrimage to our fatherland last June, for your having kissed our native soil like the hand of a beloved mother, and for your blessing of peace. You have shown the way to lasting peace for the fatherland. We thank you for the courage with which you have tackled all the problems through which we are living. You said at the Belvedere Palace that agreement in the nation can only be attained by the maintenance of the advantages acquired in August 1980—by accepting and respecting them—and not by the systematic elimination of everything for which the workers struggled.

We are particularly grateful to you, we who have gathered together in the church at Zoliborz in order to pray for the fatherland and those who suffer for it. For you have assured us that we are on the right road, when we pray for peace in the fatherland; for truth, love, and justice, for the strengthening of hope and the liberation of innocent prisoners; for the dignity of human work and the defense of the ideals of August 1980; and for the solidarity of hearts and minds.

We are thankful to you for the words of comfort addressed to youth on the occasion of your appeal at Jasna Gora, although we have deeply resented your inability to contact youth, which was the case in Warsaw four years ago, during your first pilgrimage to our country.

We are grateful to you for having recalled to us the words of the late, lamented, revered primate of the millenium, who said that the right of association according to professions is an innate right given by the Creator. It is conceded by no one. It is not the state that gives us this right—its duty is only to protect it and to "watch out" lest it be infringed upon and violated.

We are grateful to you for the words pronounced at Cracow, when you prayed that we be made strong by the power of faith, hope, and love, by the power of truth, liberty, and justice—we are also grateful for this.

We thank you for embracing with paternal tenderness the mother of the murdered Gregory at the Church of the

Capuchin fathers. Recently, you wrote her a short letter, in which we read, "Dear Madam: I believe with all my heart that she who experienced most deeply the sorrow of the loss of her beloved son is the one who understands you. She will help you in your desire to be yourself and live for others. . ."

Last month, when the worker Lech Walesa won the Nobel Peace Prize, you saw in this distinction—as did all your fellow countrymen who love the country—the fact that this award was intended for the entire nation because of its marvelous attitude during a time of humiliation, lies, and injustice. In a telegram, you wrote joyful words of warm congratulations and stressed "thus have been rewarded the will and the efforts taken to resolve the difficult problems of the world of the worker and of Polish society by the peaceful route of sincere dialogue and the mutual collaboration of all."

O Holy Father even though you sent some good wishes to Poland from the Vatican, there were still people to be found who, with incomprehensible stubbornness, never ceased attacking and humiliating the laureate and failed to realize that in doing so they were humiliating the entire working world and reducing the possibility for achieving sincere dialogue and national agreement to next to nothing.

We remember the day on which the world was shocked and absolutely amazed by the announcement of the attempt against your life—May 13, 1981. Throughout that night the churches in Warsaw and other cities were packed with people praying for your speedy recovery.

The steelworkers of Warsaw immediately set up an improvised altar in front of their mills; they festooned it with a banner on which they had written "Holy Father, we are praying for you" and, kneeling on the pavement, they participated in holy mass celebrated for your intention.

True to form, true to your goodness that we admire, when the time came, you pardoned the one who, armed with a pistol, made an attempt upon your life because you knew that he was only a blind instrument between the hands of Satan acting from afar.

We are grateful to you, Holy Father, for each of your expressions of good will, for each of your words, for each of your personal reprimands. We thank you for having answered one of our fellow countrymen living abroad who deplored the fickleness of the "extremists" in Solidarity who had "rocked the boat": "Ah, these extremists among us, these Kosciuszkos, these Pilsudskis. . ."

We thank you for imitating Christ in love without silencing your rightful indignation. For weren't you, like Christ, devouring the hypocrisy of the Pharisees with firmness when you reacted to the article in which a functionary of a friendly state wrote with cynicism: "It appears that John Paul also is calling for peace but we have difficulty in believing it given the fact that he doesn't rely upon the pacifist movement"? You responded on the first occasion that we don't have the right to confuse peace with blind obedience to force, with intimidation, or with the repression of man and the nation. A real patriot is simply one who concedes the right to patriotism to other nations.

You said once at Castelgandolfo that you were very moved each time when, on television, you saw the populace placing the cross of flowers on Victory Plaza near the Church of Saint Anne. Today we deplore, as you do, that even this joy is being refused you. Instead of crosses or flowers, Victory Plaza is still being repaired, and there are reenforced patrols stationed near the Church of Saint Anne.

We follow each of your pilgrimages, Holy Father, and we watch other countries, not always Catholic, having the opportunity to travel with you and hear your words on television. Even though you belong to our native land and we should have a right to follow your travels, this is not permitted.

We often ask ourselves why, for example, in Rio de Janeiro, they put up a plaque commemorating the spot on which you knelt to embrace the soil of Brazil—yes, why in so many places in the world except in your own country? We recall all of that today, now that five years of your pontificate have been completed. We recall it in order to better understand what an extraordinary gift was received from God, for the world and for the Fatherland, in your person, John Paul II.

We beg you today never to cease interceding for our country, in which there are always so many injustices, in which people remain in prison, without any trial, because of holding to a proscribed opinion while the guilty enjoy freedom; for our Fatherland, in which there are so many troubles and lies; for our Fatherland, in which despite everything, hope is affirmed, and solidarity of hearts and minds among men of good will is being developed.

We beg you finally, our beloved Holy Father, as did those prisoners mentioned earlier: "Be with us, be with us in prayer and in your heart, as we are always with you."

Amen.

NOVEMBER 1983

Homily
In spite of the intention of those who condemned him, the death of Jesus Christ on the cross was not a defeat, but a victory. The blood of Christ on the cross was not a defeat but a victory. The blood of Christ, poured forth on the cross, became a source of salvation. For humanity it made possible the return to the house of the Father, to the kingdom of heaven, the kingdom of truth, of love, of justice, and of peace. Upon all of those who had concluded a convenant with him through the Sacrament of Baptism, Jesus Christ imposed the duty of building up the kingdom founded on these principles.

The Polish nation, united for more than a thousand years with Christ and with his teaching, was always faithful to God, to the church and to the fatherland. The motto "God and Fatherland" had always been inseparable from the history of our nation. The Polish people always knew how to unite the sacrifice of life with the suffering and sacrifice of Jesus Christ in order that by this union nothing might be lost, but rather would become a source of nourishment for generations to come.

Great were the sufferings of the Polish nation, and much blood was shed in the course of its history, especially at the time of partition and on the occasions of revolts and national uprisings. Great were the sufferings of the nation during World War II especially during the Warsaw uprising.

The sufferings of our nation did not end after World War II. They did not end after the black years, the death camps, after the loss of millions of human lives in the Nazi and Soviet concentration camps.

Our people began to lift the country out of the ruins

of war. Poland looked toward a better future with hope but did so through its tears—not only because it had poured out much of its blood and had suffered much but also because this country, which had participated in the end of the war as a conqueror, had lost a third of its territory. The entire populace has never recovered from this "rape of the nation." Our nation made a great sacrifice by suffering and pouring out its blood after the war: the sacrifice is all the greater in that it was perpetrated with the hands of contemporary Cains, born and bred on the same native soil.

There is no need to enumerate all the sufferings of the nation since the war. Our most merciful God knows all of that.

But let us at least mention some of them. The nation suffered when the best sons of the Resistance and of the Army of the Interior were dragged before courts, tortured, and beaten in the course of being questioned, and condemned to long prison terms; there were many death sentences, and very often the sentences were carried out.

The church also suffered. Priests and bishops found themselves thrown into prison. The struggle against the church became part of the struggle against the nation. The late lamented primate of Poland, Cardinal Stefan Wyszynski, spent some years in prison because he defended the essential rights of the human person. This great man tried, oftentimes against all odds, to follow the gospel principle of rendering to Ceasar what is Caesar's and to God what is God's. But he could no longer continue to remain silent when Caesar attempted to appropriate for himself more and more of what belonged to God, namely, consciences and human souls.

When the cup of bitterness was full, the people rose up to protest.

In 1956 at Poznan the workers cried out: "We want bread, we want freedom, we want religion," and they were turned upon for this very reason. The innocent blood of our brothers flowed. Families were in mourning. There were interrogations, beatings, and arrests. But at the price of these sacrifices and of this innocent blood, the best sons of Poland were rehabilitated, many of them, unfortunately, after their deaths. It was at the price of this suffering that the primate of Poland regained his freedom.

But those responsible for the shedding of innocent blood were not punished; lessons have not been drawn from this. Their mea culpa (through my fault) was not sincere, if, only a short time afterwards, they set about mistreating the nation and the church once again. They attempted to close seminaries. They withdrew the licenses of schools of higher education in order to interrupt the studies of seminarians and to draft them for two years into the Army, into special units. They mistreated the students, several of whom had to abandon their studies. A ditch, so to speak, was dug between students and workers, between workers and intellectuals.

The sorrowful trials of the Polish millenium—those of youth in 1968 and all the other deceptions and humiliations—made the cup of suffering overflow in 1970. In this new appeal for freedom, justice, and truth, for bread and love, there were a number of dock workers at Gdansk in the forefront. Today we pay homage, we bow before our gunned-down brothers of Gdansk and Gdynia who shed their innocent blood during the tragic month of December 1970.

The nation believed the shattered declarations; it had kept confidence; but in 1976 the workers of Ursus and Radom had to demand decent living and working conditions. In response they received, in each case, insults, dismissals from jobs, and condemnations—a matter of shame for the judges but not for the condemned.

Nevertheless the sufferings of the nation proved fruitful. Nourished by fraternal blood and sorrow, a new generation appears to be enriched by the experience of the past. In August 1980 the maturity of the people, united in a common desire to build our fatherland through love, was clear for all to see. Solidarity showed that a united nation in union with God is capable of doing great things. Do not tell me that Solidarity went down in defeat. It is moving towards victory slowly, but it enjoys more and more of a base in the nation. It perhaps still needs to suffer greatly; it must yet be tested in the same way that gold is purified. But August 1980 showed the way to the new generation, to those who live in love of truth, sobriety, courage, and fraternal love.

If the authorities had actually wanted to understand the words of Cardinal Wyszynski—writing formally to the minister of worship that the real enemies of the state are those who bridle truth and those who lie—if they had wanted to understand that human life and national life are like the earth—if cockle is sewn, weeds are harvested; if good grain is sewn, truth, love, and respect for human dignity will be harvested abundantly—how greatly different Polish life could have been even in the difficult conditions of the postwar era! Unfortunately this was not to be. But let us continue our reflections.

We have already referred, on several occasions during our monthly masses for the fatherland, to the sufferings endured by the nation during martial law.

Let us be content today merely to recall the innocent death of our brothers in the Wujek mine, the death of our brothers in Lubin, in Nowa Huta, and other localities, and the brutality of the crime committed against Gregory Przemyk.

We wish to recall how human dignity was flouted and our brothers beaten. We want to recall the internment camps spread practically everywhere throughout the Polish nation and to recall the tears of mothers, of fathers, of children , of wives, and of husbands. We remember the directors of Solidarity and of KOR (Committee of Defense of the Workers) imprisoned now for two years, without a trial. We recall those who were, and are still, separated for long months from their families because they do not choose to deny their consciences through a form of conditional surrender.

We wish to recall those who were fired and who have concern for the material welfare of their families; the young who are obliged to have crosses, symbols of their faith, taken off the walls of their schoolrooms, the teachers who were let go because they wanted to transmit sound principles of patriotism to youth.

The media were employed to prepare defamatory accusations against people who enjoyed the respect of society. Let us recall the long lines waiting in front of stores, in contempt of human dignity, with tickets for food. How about also recalling those paid police informers.

On this November evening we really had to remind ourselves of the fact that we are not allowed to permit this immensity of national suffering to be lost but that we must humbly offer it to God in prayer. Too great is the tribute of blood, suffering, tears, and humiliation placed at the feet of Christ that it would not be returned to us by God in the form of the gift of true freedom, justice, and love.

This will be as much a resurrection of the fatherland to us as what took place in 1918, even though it seemed impossible that the three occupying powers would be defeated at the same time; it was humanly impossible, but God has shown us that all is possible in him.

Perhaps it will still be necessary for many more personal commitments to be made so that the sacrificial cup of the nation can be effectively filled. Perhaps there still is not enough voluntary renunciation, not enough human solidarity, not enough courage to denounce evil, not enough looking at those who suffer, those who are mistreated and imprisoned. Perhaps there is still too much egotism in us, too much upset, too much alcoholism or too many stupid people without worthwhile ideas who are careful about safeguarding their own interest and doing so at the expense of others. Perhaps there aren't enough citizens faithful to the ideals for which our brothers shed their blood?

May the month of November 1918 be a stimulus today for all of those who are upset, who are filled with fear, whose courage is waning. Let it prompt us to work, us and others, for the strengthening and the reaffirmation of hope, since in every situation God is capable of leading the nation toward freedom if the people are faithful to God, to the church, and to the fatherland, and if the people live in faith, hope, love, truth, and solidarity.

Amen.

DECEMBER 1983

Christmas Homily

On this Christmas Eve, it would be enough just to be silent, to close one's hands, to look oneself in the eye, and—in place of a sermon—to find again in oneself a spark of mutual love. It would be sufficient to see the tears of those who suffer, to open one's heart to the innocent thrown in prison and to their families, to accept the orphan, the woman too quickly deprived of the one she loves...Then it would be sufficient to sing with one voice. Yes, we will be able to "hang in there."

However, on Christmas Day, the song of the angels breaks forth: "Glory to God in the Highest, and peace on earth to men of good will," for God has confided peace to men on the night of Christmas.

Peace upon earth, peace in hearts and consciences, Peace is the good to which humanity most aspires today.

In the course of the holy masses for the fatherland and for those who suffer for it, I have never let my own voice be heard. I have let it be guided by the gospel, by the teaching of the primate of the millenium, Cardinal Stefan Wyszynski, and by that of the Holy Father, John Paul II.

Today once again in this reflection on peace, I would like, above all, to quote from the words of the Holy Father.

In his encyclical *Pacem in Terris* Pope John XXIII said that "peace must be founded upon truth, constructed according to the demands of justice, made vibrant and fulfilled by love and realized in a climate of freedom."

The Holy Father, John Paul II, in his statement for the Day of Peace, develops this truth presented by one of his predecessors. I give the floor now to the Holy Father, the greatest son of our nation:

"Peace must be based on truth." (John XXIII)

"*A renewal of truth is necessary if one wishes that individuals, groups, and nations not doubt the force of peace and accept new forms of repression. To reestablish truth implies first of all that we call by its proper name every act of repression, whatever form it takes. It is important to call a murder by its name, a murder is always a crime; political and ideological motivations incapable of transforming its nature, lose their weight.*

"*To cry out for truth, in as much as it is a force for peace, implies that we undertake ceaseless efforts to refuse to have recourse to the arm of the lie, even when the goals are laudable. . . .*

"*The Gospel strongly emphasizes the bond existing between the lie and repression. According to the words of Christ: 'Now you are attempting to kill me, I a man who told you the truth that I had heard from God. . . You do the work of your father. . . You are of the devil, your father, and these are the desires of your father that you wish to accomplish. He was a murderer from the beginning and was not rooted in truth, because there is no truth in him: when he uttered a lie, he spoke on his own behalf, because he is liar and father of lies' (John 8:40-41, 44).*

"*The vital force of Gospel peace is truth. Thus we must live the truth and then this truth will cause the light to appear to us and raise up unexpected energies, energy opening up new possibilities for peace in the world. Peace must be founded upon justice. Peace is an honest dialogue in the spirit of love.*

"*Dialogue, true dialogue is an important condition for peace. Certain interested parties are nourished by ideologies which, in spite of declarations, are contrary to the dignity of the human person and of his just aspirations: these ideologies see, in conflict, the motivating force of history, and in designating the enemy they see the source of laws. Then dialogue is threatened and becomes sterile and whenever it continues to exist it is necessarily superficial and false.*

"*It is only possible to arrive at a peaceful solution of problems by a sincere dialogue and respect for a whole roster of freedoms . . . When dialogue between the government and the nation breaks down, social peace is threatened . . . and in some way a state of war appears.*"

Thus it appears between individuals, social groups, and nations. "

"*It is important never to reject dialogue, it is important never to have recourse to armed force in order to resolve conflicts.*"

Peace must be constructed according to the principles of justice.

"*For what nations are capable of establishing, in a real way, international peace if they themselves are slaves of ideologies. Justice and peace cannot come from those who are disqualified and judged unworthy of deciding their own destiny. You who have the responsibility of nations must, by necessity yourselves, love peace.*"

If the impediments of peace are to be removed, it is not just enough that words be sincere. What follows "*are the basic and intangible elements on which it is necessary to establish oneself in order to maintain peace; the affairs of man must be considered with humanity and can never be imposed by force. Tensions, differences, and conflicts must be resolved by the balanced way of negotiation and not by repression. Ideological opposing views demand confrontation in a climate of dialogue and free discussion . . .*

"*The inalienable rights of man must be preserved in all circumstances. It is not permitted to kill in order to impose on others one or another particular solution. . .*"

Peace must be realized in a climate of freedom "*Without overall respect for freedom, man will not build peace.*

"*Freedom is restricted when relations between*

nations are established on the basis of force, when they are based on the concept of power blocks, on military or political imperialism. The freedom of nations is stifled when dialogue between partners is no longer possible because of economic or financial domination exercised by strong and privileged nations. The freedom of nations is stifled when the weak are forced to submit themselves to the strong . . .

"There is no true liberty, the sole foundation of peace, where power is concentrated between the hands of a single social class, of a single race, of a single group and whenever the common good is identified with the interests of a single party which is identified with the state . . .

"Man is truly free who strives to promote the liberty of others. To be free is to live according to one's conscience. Freedom of conscience and of religion is the basic inalienable right of the human person . . .

"A society built exclusively on materialistic foundations withholds freedom from man when individual liberties are subordinated to the economy, when it smothers the spiritual creation of man in the name of a false ideological system, when it denies people the right to associate freely together, when it rules out, in practice, the right of participating in public life . . .

"To be free of fear, of injustice, of.repression, of suffering is to no avail if deep down man remains a slave. The Christian finds the strength to struggle for freedom and peace when he places his hope in God."

Such are the essential words of the Holy Father, John Paul II.

In 1963 the Polish bishop, led by the late lamented primate, wrote in a pastoral letter:

"Those who have brought down upon the earth
this immense suffering and woe and those who
have plunged the world into the abyss of wars
have struggled principally against His Church

because they know that the Christian religion is
the main obstacle to their endeavors."

Let us end these reflections today with the words of
the primate of the millenium, who declared in his message
of Christmas 1980:

"Let the fire of war, let devilish armaments, let
nuclear explosions no longer terrorize us. Let
military pageants cease, let stockpiles of arms
become stockpiles of grain so that we can build
hospitals and schools and so that the pretext of
defending peace with armaments will end. Such
a way is not the road toward the peace and
tranquility of human hearts."

Let us meditate upon the words of the encyclical
Pacem in Terris to which I referred in the beginning:
"Peace must be founded upon truth, constructed
according to the demands of justice, made vibrant and
fulfilled by love, and realized in a climate of freedom";
and let us live each day in the spirit of the gospel that a
newborn child brought to us 1,983 years ago in a stable
at Bethlehem that Christmas night. Amen.

*Statement of Father Jerzy Popieluszko Read in Church
December 18, 1983.*

Given the events that have concerned me these days,
and given the publication of information regarding a
search that was made of my apartment, and not having any
other possibility for telling it as it is, I am obliged to inform
the faithful in the following manner:

I own only a modest apartment that was offered to me
by my aunt five years ago. My ecclesiastical authorities
have been informed of this.

Some objects have been found in this apartment.
Where they came from is totally unknown to me and in
the light of my known pastoral activity on behalf of the
faithful, the nature of these objects is absolutely absurd.

I view this as a provocation.

1984

JANUARY 1984

Homily
"God so loved the world that He gave His only Son so that any man who believes in Him may not die but possess life eternal" (John 3:16).

God so loved man that He made His child one whom He lifted up to the dignity of a child of God.

Are we taking sufficient account of this great distinction that is divine sonship? Are we taking sufficient account of this dignity given by God? Just as freedom is not only given but ordained, so too is human dignity. It is ordained for us throughout our entire lives. And it is up to us to preserve this gift of dignity as children of God until the end of our earthly pilgrimage.

The following is an example of a man who with all his heart, served God, his family, and his fatherland and who was able to preserve his dignity right up until the very end; I speak of General Romuald Traugutt (1825–1864), the most renowned leader of the January 1863 insurrection. (There is currently serious talk of beatifying him.) The late lamented primate of the millenium once said of him: "He taught us to join love of the fatherland to love of God."

He united the love of God with love of the fatherland when he wrote in a letter to General Jozef Hauke Bosak: "The Polish soldier must be a true soldier of Christ; he must spread, far and wide, purity of conduct and immaculate virtue and not lawlessness and demoralization."

He united love of God with love of the fatherland when he testified before the Russian Military Commission of Inquiry: "The only real purpose of our insurrection is the recovery of independence and the establishment in our country of an order founded upon Christian love, upon respect for law and every aspect of justice.''

He united love of God with love of the fatherland when he explained his accession to the highest level of power thusly: "Only an unlimited confidence in Providence and an unmovable faith in the sacred character of our cause gave me the strength and the courage to accept, under these conditions, power which was in jeopardy. I remembered that power is an act of sacrifice and not of ambition.''

He united the love of God and fatherland when he wrote to Pope Pius IX: "Moscow realizes that it will not break down Catholic Poland; that is why Moscow vents its fury on the pastors of our souls.''

He preserved his dignity when life did not spare him various trials and when God, in a period of less than two years, had taken five persons who were particularly dear to him.

He preserved his dignity when he addressed himself to the peoples of Europe: "It is not appropriate to moan or grovel while addressing the one who stands up as a defender of the trampled and rejected rights of humanity, the one who has struggled without arms for more than a year, with unflinching confidence in Most Holy Justice, against the furious enemy, without taking count of the number of his forces and of his hordes, but counting solely upon the sacredness of the cause and upon the principles which he defends.''

It was almost axiomatic with him that it is worth more to suffer out of zeal for the things of God than to see oneself the recipient of praise from enemies of God and of the church.

He preserved his dignity when, full of peace and serenity and accepting the divine will with genuine Christian courage, he offered his life in sacrifice for love upon the altar of the fatherland. The inhabitants of Warsaw deeply appreciated him for the tremendous valor of his action: a crowd of ten thousand persons gathered together at the foot of the citadel praying and singing: "Holy God, Mighty God . . ."

Romuald Traugutt is an example for us of a Pole who esteemed it his personal duty not to spare himself when others had sacrificed everything. Here was a Pole who understood that anyone who wished to devote himself to his fatherland could not neglect God. He had to collaborate with God.

The January insurrection once more confirmed that physical force alone, however mighty it may be, cannot honestly and lastingly resolve the problems of the state. The might of the czars did put down the insurrection, but it could not put down the aspiration of the Polish nation to live in truth and justice, in freedom and love.

It is essential to live one's life worthily since it is unique. "It is important to speak a great deal today about the eminent dignity of man in order to understand that man surpasses everything which can exist in the world, with the exception of God, who surpasses the wisdom of the entire world" (Cardinal Wyszynski).

To preserve one's dignity as man is to remain free within, even when slavery exists outside. To continue to be yourself, to live in truth is the bare minimum necessary for guaranteeing that one's image as a child of God not be erased.

The career of every man on earth, the late lamented primate declared, "began in diapers. Even if today he wears the uniform of an ambassador or of a general, his career will end up in a winding sheet of perhaps a little larger size." That is why it is not enough to be born a man. It is more important still, to live as a man.

To preserve one's dignity as man is to continue to be one's self in all situations of life. It is to preserve the truth even if this is going to cost us dearly. For to speak the truth can cost a great deal. Only the weed is given away; we must pay for the grain of truth. Every great cause has its price and is meant to be difficult. Only ordinary and unimportant things come easily. The poet Novalis once said "Man depends on truth. If he betrays truth, he betrays himself. He who betrays truth, betrays himself." The lie debases human dignity and is the sole prerogative of slaves, of the weak.

Last February the Holy Father declared, "You are not a slave. You do not have the right to be a slave. You are a son of God."

To preserve one's dignity is to live in accord with one's conscience. It involves awakening and forming a correct conscience in one's self.

It involves watching over the national conscience, for we know that when the national conscience fails, great evils plague our history. Nevertheless, when the national conscience begins to be awakened and to become alive due to a sense of responsibility for the land of our birth, then the renewal of the nation ensues. So it was on the occasions of revolutionary uprisings; so it was on the occasion of the January uprising; so it was during the time of Solidarity. "Poles" (I am again quoting from the late lamented primate) "have to struggle for the good order of their fatherland, out of a sense of duty, for the peace of God, and for the right to enjoy the freedom which is due all of us." We must cultivate in ourselves this capacity for struggle if we wish to remain a nation that, in spite of the cross on its shoulders, is moving with dignity toward the resurrection.

True freedom is the basic constitutive element of humanity. It is a special sign of the image of God in man. It has been given to us by God, offered not only to us but also to our brothers. This implies that we have the duty of winning it for those who are unjustly deprived of it.

To preserve one's dignity as man, one's dignity as a child of God, is to live without lying. Do not be lukewarm!

"How many men are there in Poland," asked the primate of the millenium, "who make themselves out to be atheists out of fear or cowardice? This is a terrible wound to the human psyche; it will have some serious consequences and bad effects in the future."

You will not preserve your full dignity by carrying around the rosary in one pocket and a little book of a totally opposite ideology in the other. You cannot, at one and the same time, serve God and Mammon. You cannot serve two masters at one and the same time. You must make a choice—but go forward only after mature reflection.

In every man there is a trace of God. Look to see, brother, if you haven't rubbed too much of it out of yourself. Whatever may be your profession, you are a man. Being a man is of inestimable value.

In 1938 some police officers came on pilgrimage to Jasna Gora. Upon the ex-voto that they offered to the Mother of God, they had inscribed: "The faith of our ancestors and of our fathers is ours; it will be that of our children and grandchildren." Preserve your dignity because you are a man—whatever your profession. Work is for man and not man for work, just as man's welfare demands that the regime be for man and not man for the regime.

God never abandons his children, even those who turn their back on him. Get a hold of yourself, reassess your situation, lift yourself up. Begin again. Try to build up what is godlike in yourself. Try, for you have but one life.

Finally, human dignity is also the dignity of human work. It is the right to have conditions conducive to work so that the energies of man are not worn out and man himself is not prematurely burned out. The most important thing is not that man produce a great many things in a short time but that he work well. Man can be humiliated; he can also be deprived of his dignity through work when, by the sheer dint of external pressures, he is spurred on to the limit of his efforts—thereby violating the order decreed by God. Purely materialistic civilization makes man a slave of his own productions and it deprives him of his real worth.

We must not forget this truth: in order to preserve faith and dignity, we can sacrifice even our own freedom, but in order to preserve freedom we do not have the right to sacrifice our faith and dignity as children of God.

In August 1982 the Holy Father prayed as follows: "May the heart of our Mother bring it about that we never renounce efforts for truth and justice, for freedom and the dignity of our lives."

Let us therefore stay on the road of truth and freedom, on the road of the fundamental rights of man, on the road of respect for conscience, on the road of solidarity with our brothers unjustly condemned, on the road of safeguarding our human dignity and divine sonship.

May the all-powerful God and she who is our Queen and our Mother help us to keep ourselves on that road.

Amen.

FEBRUARY 1984

Homily

"Suffer the little children to come unto me and do not hinder them." These words, spoken by Christ the Lord in the gospel had the same meaning for two thousand years. They have special relevance for our history. They have even greater relevance today.

We are children of the nation who, for more than a thousand years, have sung the glory of the One God in Three Persons. Our nation was world-renowned for its religious toleration. Those who had to leave their homeland because of religious persecutions, found a place with us.

In the Polish nation, Christian education was deeply rooted in the history of the fatherland, and it exercised its influence upon all other areas of life. And that is why, in present-day education, it cannot be removed from a tradition that characterized Poland for a thousand years. We must neither eliminate it nor deform it.

The Christian system of education, based on Christ and on his gospel, has known many trials in the course of our national history, especially during its most difficult moments.

That is why the Catholic population of Poland is conscious of the destructive moral prejudices that have been imposed upon believers, even to the point of seeking to establish a program of atheistic education hostile to religion.

Since World War II, there has been a succession of struggles in behalf of a monopoly for atheistic education, education without God, the eradication of God from the hearts of children and young people.

Let us now look at today's problem a little more closely.

The life of a child begins in the heart of its mother. It is the mother who assumes the greatest responsibility, first of all in bringing the child into the world and then, with its father, in educating the child. In the process of education, the school and society also participate together. However, in its work the school necessarily has to depend upon the parents. The school must not destroy, in the souls of children, the values that have been inculcated by the family.

"The school is national and it belongs to the nation, to the family, and to society, and not to one or another particular group, party or sect, that involves itself in an activity that is hostile and counter-productive to the nation and to the state and that is aimed at eliminating faith from the hearts of children and of young people," the late lamented primate, Cardinal Stefan Wyszynski, used to state.

Therefore, in spite of the public nature of the school, it must serve the family and the nation because the nation is comprised of families. The school must be national. It must enkindle in children and young people a love of the fatherland and of national culture. The school must take the nation into consideration, its needs, its culture, its customs, its religion.

The duty of promoting such a school, of keeping watch to guarantee a suitable education, reposes in the state, the teachers, and parents. But when the state neglects this duty, a much greater responsibility devolves on the parents and teachers. Worse yet is the situation that, under the guise of new educational projects and under the pretext of discharging parents from education, of the children, struggles to achieve a monopoly in education, and atheistic instruction, contrary to the will of parents.

The program of "atheistation" leads to absurdity; it provokes a feeling of social violence and of personal repression.

"The shame of our times," the bishops wrote in 1968, is that there are numerous attempts aimed at depriving young people of faith in God and of a relationship with the church, contrary to the voice of conscience among all civilized nations. Laws and decrees, especially those that concern education, cannot contradict divine law, for then they would not bind in conscience; but the repression of man is produced when an outlook on life that deprives him of the freedom of believing and loving God is imposed upon him. He is alienated from all his hopes and from all his religious desires."

It could be objected that no one today hinders people from going to Church. This, however, is what we have experienced since the war. Today many adults are asking to be baptized because their parents feared losing their jobs if they baptized their children or if they sent them to catechism classes.

But the problems of education and religious freedom are not limited to practice. The regime can impose neither its religion nor its outlook on life. It cannot dictate what citizens must or must not believe.

Isn't putting restrictions on a Catholic press in a Catholic country, where a secular press has proliferated to millions of copies while there exist only a few Catholic weeklies with ridiculously low press runs, tantamount to imposing an atheistic religion and being deficient in toleration?

One of the causes of our contemporary material and moral misfortunes is that Christ's place in the education of children and young people, notably at school and at work, has been consistently challenged.

In the recent past we went through a period in which summer camp counselors, in the name of a presumed freedom of conscience, were forbidden to bring the children to mass each Sunday. They were advised to organize activities at the very time when masses were being celebrated in the Churches and, finally, the counselors were forbidden to allow the children to go to Mass even if they asked to do so. Students and counselors were threatened, and those who broke these rules were severely penalized. This was a radical violation of the rights of man. School principals were required to give reports regarding their activities aimed at making the children's participation in catechism more difficult and at influencing parents in order to emphasize the destructive nature of religious education.

Teachers who facilitated children's attendance at catechism classes were threatened with severe penalties.

Young people were threatened; attendance at catechism classes made it impossible for them to pass the baccalaureate exams and gain access to higher studies. (A number of bishops have written about this in their pastoral letters.) I am recalling this affair in order to stress the major importance of the family in education; for it was first and foremost the parents' function to clear up all the confusion created in the minds of their children—whether the children were believers or if during the time of Solidarity, being of the generation raised in these difficult times, searching for the strength and support of God and the Church.

Consequently, when the state is not on top of its duties the responsibility of parents, teachers, and youth themselves is that much heavier.

Youth must see in the teacher a friend who, first and foremost, speaks the truth and who tries to transmit to the younger generation everything that has been received from national and religious culture. Teachers must remember the fact that they are educating youth for the fatherland, whose roots are deeply embedded in a glorious past. They are not educating youth for any one of a number of regimes that will come and go.

Young people run the risk of losing their connection

with the national past and with Polish culture (now often ridiculed and misrepresented)—a danger recently halted by Solidarity which has corrected many historical facts consciously passed over in silence. We are not a nation only for today; we are a nation that must transmit, over the long haul, the riches that have been accumulating in the course of a thousand years. Only the mutual, harmonious collaboration of parents, teachers, the church, and young people themselves can counteract what is intended to play down the human goodness and reduce to nothing the heritage of sacrifices by whole generations of Poles who paid a very high price to maintain the spirit of the nation.

Therefore, we must all take to heart the appeal of the primate of the millenium, who invited us to have the courage to confess publicly Christ and the church, as well as everything that constitutes the glory of the nation. We are to have the courage to recognize Christ in school, university, factory, and office. It is only fitting that we do this without taking into account the repercussions that can result for us. If we are believers, we can do this between the four walls of our homes; but let us not be lacking in courage to confess Christ in public, even if it means our having to pay the price and make sacrifices.

Our faith and our ideals cannot be sold for a mess of porridge, for a job, for a higher salary, for the possibility of studying, for social advancement. The person who sells his faith and his ideals to the highest bidder is a fit candidate for selling out his brother. The Church will always give assistance to parents and teachers: its point of view is that if some people have the right to propagate atheism against the nation's will, against the will of Catholic parents and of young people themselves, Catholics possess much more of a right to defend themselves against the incursions of the law.

We speak much today of the rights of man, and we

often forget the basic right to religious liberty and to freedom in education. The state forgets, when it sometimes transforms itself into an apostle of faith in what it calls its god, which is called atheism or secularism, that it is ordering the entire nation to bow before a god made in accordance with its own specifications. Only the concerted effort of the church, of parents, and of educators, demonstrating proof of that healthy patriotism that has been part and parcel of our nation for more than ten centuries, can prevent our youth from going down blind alleys.

We must do everything that is possible in our power to protect the mouths of our children, our young people, or the nation from being shut.

Let us not lose heart!

The czar once declared, "Poles, abandon all hope, shut your mouths." They didn't do so and, as a result, they paid dearly; but they did not let themselves be silenced, and today we are indebted to them because they are the ones who handed down our national spirit to us. We are the inheritors of those who have not "shut up," since we continue to deal with a number of important questions facing the nation. Thus we, ourselves, must not be silent when it is a question of the education of the young generation that will soon bear on its shoulders the destiny of its native land.

My dear young friends, you must have within yourselves qualities similar to those of eagles[1]—an eagle's heart and an eagle's eye, as the late lamented primate once said. You must harden your soul and lift it high in order to be able, like the eagles, to soar above the flock as you move forward to the future of our fatherland. It is only by resembling eagles that you will be able, without letting yourselves be led into slavery, to withstand the winds, storms, and tempests of history. Remember this! Eagles are free

---

[1]The national emblem of Poland is a white eagle.

birds, since they fly high in the heavens and do not scrawl about on the ground.

But, can you be like the eagles? That depends upon those whom you allow to form your souls and your minds, by recalling to you that loyal citizens cannot be mass-produced in factories but must be formed by the heart of mothers and the true educators who find the model for a good teacher residing in Jesus Christ.

Amen.

MARCH 1984

Homily

Very Holy Mother, we gather together each month in this church at Zoliborz to celebrate holy Mass for the fatherland and for those who suffer the most for her. Today, the Holy Father, John Paul II, is entrusting the entire world, all people and nations, to you; and we place before your blessed hands, you the best of Mothers, all the problems of our fatherland, for which we have been praying these last years.

Allow us to recall some of these to you and to confide them to you once again.

To you, the best of Mothers, we entrust first of all our brothers imprisoned for opinions offensive to the regime, imprisoned for having had the courage to think in another fashion than that which is imposed. They have been imprisoned for more than two years, without trial, without verdict. These are the members of the board of directors of Solidarity. If they are guilty, why haven't they been judged? And we are well aware that only those who have democratically elected them should have the right to judge them. Millions of Poles should alone be able to judge them; for millions of citizens, they continue to be a symbol of the genuine freedom of the fatherland.

We believe that their suffering will bear excellent fruit. We believe it, as they believe it, especially when they write these words: "Today more than ever we see the necessity of sacrifice for a cause as great as that undertaken in August 1980. We know that without fire we cannot bend a rod of steel but we ourselves have such great need of being bent." We entrust to you all the prisoners of Warsaw, of Barczew, of Braniew, of Strzelin, and of Lubiniec. They are frequently treated worse then common criminals.

It was from the prison of Lubliniec that Anna Walentynowicz wrote, "The sorrow of my absence, and not only mine, the loss of freedom, this is what gives reality to the words of the Holy Father: 'Peace be to you, Poland.'"

We place our confidence in you and we entreat you, Mother of innocent prisoners, come to their assistance.

To you we entrust Polish youth, the future and the hope of the nation, who are constantly deprived of conditions conducive to the development of their personalities in accordance with their own freely chosen values. They are also refused the opportunity to develop socially in youth organizations that correspond to their own convictions.

We entrust to you the youth at the Garwolin agricultural school who have shown so much courage and maturity in defending the continued presence of crucifixes in their classrooms. The voice of the young people in Garwolin is that of all young believers in Poland, those who understand that in struggling for the right to keep the crucifix in the classroom they are struggling for respect for the constitutional principle of freedom of worship and of conscience. The behavior of the school authorities, however, is a new attempt to enslave the spirit of the nation. The school is for the pupils, not the pupils for the school—in the same way as a regime must be at the service of the nation and not the nation at the service of the regime. No believer wants to hang up the cross in places where there are nonbelievers, but believers do have the right to decide for themselves if they want to have the crucifix in their work places.

We entrust unto you, O Mother of Christ, the bitterness of powerlessness and humiliation to which so many brothers and sisters in our fatherland are continually being subjected.

We entrust unto you the sorrow and the bitterness of the former prisoners of Darlowek and of Jaworz. Wishing at the time of their release to thank the priests of the area for their pastoral zeal at the internment camps, they donated a totally religious banner with your image, Mary, and that of your faithful servant Maximilian Kolbe. On the way they encountered barricades: the majority of the internees was challenged and taken into custody at the very moment of the solemn transmission of the banner, which was then seized by the security police.

We entrust unto you the painful and still current affair of the trial of Gregory Przemyk's murderers. The injustice is all the more sorrowful because, for one whole year, there has been no arrest of those who fired the shots while on duty—yet it is so easy to bring accusations against those defendants who are in conformity with truth.

At this moment we especially entrust to you, best of Mothers, the lawyer Bednarkiewicz, now imprisoned, whose nobility and uprightness you know so well.

We entrust to you the glorious word *Solidarity* and all that it evokes in the minds of Poles.

Since the dissolution of Solidarity and of the union, it has become a synonym for the nation. To battle against the nation is to fight windmills. No one will be able to conquer this idea Solidarity, for it is firmly anchored in the hearts of millions. An important price has been paid, the price of blood, of tears, of hiding, of prison.

We entrust unto you all the wrongs committed in the nation since World War II, chiefly during the course of these last three years of the nation's slavery. These wrongs, especially the moral wrongs and those about which we have so often spoken during our holy masses for the fatherland, cry out for reparation. At the end of this prayer, inspired by concern for our country, we entrust unto you hope for a better future—hope for peace and harmony of the nation through love, but also in the spirit of justice, because we are well aware that love cannot exist without justice.

Mother of hope, you know much better than we our daily prayers often uttered in tears. You know the sorrows and the uncertainties of our tormented hearts.

In this day in which we entrust the entire world to you and to your immaculate heart, we place all of this between your mother's hands and pray you to place them at the feet of your Son, Jesus Christ. On behalf of our fatherland, we beg you for the resurrection of genuine freedom, justice, and peace. Amen.

APRIL 1984
Monsignor Kraszewski, auxiliary bishop, gave the homily in April 1984 while visiting the parish of Saint Stanislas Kostka.

MAY 1984

Homily

On the occasion of the trial of Jesus Christ, so inglorious for the whole of humanity. Pilate asked him a question which was, is, and always will be current: "What is truth?"

For the Christian the response to this question is simple enough. It was given by Jesus Christ himself when he said: "I am the Way, the Truth and the Life." Christ is, therefore, the truth. And everything that he proclaims is the Truth. The Big Lie never slipped from his lips. He gave his life for the truth, which he proclaimed with courage. The Apostles, for whom Jesus Christ became the sole truth, gave their lives for him by courageously proclaiming his teachings throughout the world. Truth and courage are very important values in the life of each person and especially in each Christian. I would like today to attempt to spell out the implication of these two values in our lives.

Truth is a particularly subtle gift of the human spirit. It is God himself who has inculcated in man this attraction for the truth. It follows that in every person there is a natural inclination to truth and an aversion to lying. Truth is always bound to love, and love is demanding; true love requires sacrifices, and truth itself must also exact a price. Truth that costs nothing is a lie.

To live in truth is to be in agreement with one's conscience. Truth unites and binds people together. The importance of truth intimidates and unmasks the lies of the mediocre and of the fearful. The uninterrupted struggle for truth continues through the centuries. Moreover, truth is immortal and the Big Lie dies a speedy death. Let us listen to the words of Cardinal Wysznski:

It is difficult enough that a few people speak the

truth. Christ chose a small number to proclaim his truth. Only lying words demand many at their service, since a lie must be elaborate in every detail if it is to be minted and coined. It is sold like merchandise on a shelf and it must be constantly replenished. It needs many servants who, following a strict program, teach it for today or tomorrow or for a month. In order to master the technique of the programmed Big Lie, a great number of people are needed. Only a few are needed to proclaim the truth.

Only a small group of people is necessary in the struggle to allow the truth to shine forth. People find themselves in need, and they come from near and far to listen to the words of truth.

We cannot accept the trite superficial truths, those of propaganda and those that are imposed by violence. This cannot satisfy us. We must learn to distinguish the lie from the truth. This is not easy during the period in which we are living, a period about which a contemporary poet wrote: "Never has the back been so cruelly beaten by the rod of the lie and of hypocrisy." It is not easy today cause, during recent decades, the seeds of the lie and of atheism were officially being sown on our native soils. Seeds of secularism have also been sown; this view of the world is a caricatured product of capitalism and nineteenth-century freemasonry. These seeds have been sown in a country that has been solidly anchored in Christianity for more than a thousand years.

Each of us present here could cite several examples of that which forms an obstacle to the advance of truth and charity in our society. Let us examine at least a few of them.

The lie and the half-truth, which come to us especially through the mass media, do not favor the development of truth. Television programming based solely on official propaganda and secular morality, as if there were no Christians living in Poland, is no longer acceptable. Moreover, believers have a right to religious films and to Bible-based discussions. They have a right, by means of the television screen, to follow the activities of the Holy Father, who is the glory of this nation.

Censorship, which directs its attention not against evil but against the common good, is not conducive to the development of truth. This is proved in the censoring of Catholic journals with respect to the words of the Holy Father and our primate.

The primate of the millenium, of venerated memory, stated:

The censorship of periodicals and magazines is arbitrary and significant. Whatever is most Catholic, holy, powerful, and convincing . . . is cut or abbreviated. Only the Catholic finds himself forbidden to propagate his own ideas. He is forbidden to take issue with opposite ideas, to polemicize, and he is even deprived of the simple right of defending his opinions in the face of the most defamatory and unjust attacks. We cannot gain the upper hand over lies which others have the right to utter and spread with total impunity. Here is a concrete example: *Tygodnik Powszechny* of May 20 contains twenty-three cases of censorship.[1]

It is not the imposition of materialistic ideas by every conceivable means of propaganda and the presentation of Marxism as the sole means of resolving the problems of the workers that serves the truth. I will cite here once again Cardinal Wyszynski's statement of June 1980: "We must know that the hope of finding solutions to the problems of the workers is presently being

[1]   A major Catholic weekly published in Cracow and noted for its courage and forcefulness.

diminished. The total inability of the regime is clear and it can be seen in the fact that Marxism is reconstructing capitalism making man dependent upon the system of production, thereby once again taking away his freedom. Truth will not be served by blackening everything acquired by Solidarity nor by showing it under weak light, any more than it will by eradicating all traces of Solidarity in every possible way. The nation knows that in this word, a word defined recently by the Holy Father as a glorious word, the hopes and the disappointments of millions of Poles find their concrete expression.

It is not by imprisoning people for their opinions that the development of truth will be served. Come now, if the leaders of Solidarity and their brothers were imprisoned for having lied, would the church be expending so many efforts to seek their freedom and to defend them?

Repression and the shows of force do not serve truth. Repression is really deceptive, since it destroys what it pretends to defend. In order to govern a country it is necessary to renounce violence and the lie, then work to restore once again that calm and those conditions conducive to a productive building of the nation but calm should not be confused with imposed silence.

Just as one cannot fool the earth, so life cannot be fooled. If we sow weeds, we reap weeds.

The gospel of Christ, so fruitful over the centuries, is always relevant since it is the truth. Ideologies inspired by the lie and by repression come and go. They bear bad fruit and destroy morality. We have just too many examples in European and world history.

The essential condition for the liberation of man—if he is to be allowed to live in truth—is to acquire the virtue of courage. Struggle for truth is the symbol of Christian courage. The virtue of courage is a victory even over weakness, a victory over fear and cowardice, for the only thing worth fearing is betraying Christ for a few *denarii*, for a fleeting peace and quiet.

It is not sufficient for a Christian merely to condemn the lie, laziness, slavery, hatred, and repression; a Christian must be a true witness, a defender and promoter of justice, goodness, truth, freedom, and love. He must, for himself and others, lay claim to these values with courage. "Only a courageous man can be truly just and wise. Woe to the society whose citizens are not guided by courage. They then cease to be citizens and become merely slaves. Even if fear and cowardice help a person to secure a few crumbs of bread and some minor advantages, if a citizen renounces the virtue of courage, he becomes a slave and inflicts the greatest evils on himself and his person as well as his family, his professional group, and the nation, the state and the church" (John Paul II).

And again, "Woe to the rulers who want to buy off citizens at the price of fear and servile cowardice. If the regime governs frightened citizens, it exhausts its own authority and it impoverishes the national cultural life and the values of professional life" (Cardinal Wyszynski). Concern for courage should necessarily be on the same level of priority for the regime as it is for the citizen.

We are, in a large measure, to blame for our own slavery, when out of fear or accommodation we accept evil: we even support its activity. If we support its activity out of accommodation or fear, then we lose the right even to point out evil for we have become its creatures and have contributed to making it legal and reputable.

The workers passed the examination of their courage in August 1980, and some continue to pass it.

By courageously coming to the defense of the cross of Christ, the students of Mietno proved their own courage.

Our imprisoned brothers successfully passed their own examination of courage recently. They didn't choose freedom at the price of betraying their and our ideals.

Finally, let this serve as a warning to each of us! Be aware that the nation perishes when she lacks courage, when she lies to herself by saying that all goes well when all is going poorly and when she is content with half-truths.

Be aware that in demanding truth, we ourselves must live in truth; may this awareness go with us each day. In calling for justice, let us be just toward our neighbors. In calling for courage, let us each day be courageous.

Amen.

JUNE 1984

Homily

Today's liturgy speaks to us of the person of John the Baptist, the man who was originally described by the prophet Isaiah as "a voice crying in the wilderness." The man who prepared human hearts for an encounter with the one who was to come: Jesus Christ. We see in John the Baptist a courageous and just man who had the courage to condemn the evil and injustice of a king who had taken the wife of his brother. John the Baptist, this courageous and just man, can become the patron saint and the model of all those who would seek to base their lives upon principles of justice, truth, and love.

A just man is one who is guided by truth and by love. For the more truth and love are in man, the more there is justice. Justice goes along with love. Without love we cannot be fully just. When love and goodness are lacking, then hatred and violence fill in the void. A person is never just if he or she is guided by hatred and violence. In countries where power depends not upon duty and love but upon violence and repression, injustice is experienced in a particularly doleful manner. Justice based upon love is a condition of peace in our consciences and families, in the fatherland, and in the entire world. All of us, without exception, long for peace. But it is impossible to preserve peace with words alone, however sincere and bereft of demogogery. Therefore, in order that peace and calm return to the country and in order to create conditions for a happy and productive life in our community, it is first of all necessary to eliminate everything that the Nation resents as social injustice. There are just too many personal and social injuries due to the fact that justice is not on a par with love; it is on the wane; in short, there is nothing else but downright injustice.

Let us examine some of the more blatant and evident manifestations of this injustice. Being conscious that God is the very source of justice is essential to a Christian. Therefore, it is difficult to speak of justice when a person no longer respects either God or his commandments. It is justice itself that obliges us to become aware of the pain and suffering to which our nation, with its Christian majority, is being subjected, as every effort—including financial means furnished by Christians—is used to make it officially atheistic.

Justice forbids the destruction, in the souls of children and young people, of Christian values learned from parents, values that have been tried and proven throughout our one thousand-year history. To render justice and to clamor for justice is the duty of all; Plato once said, "When justice is silent, times are bad." Justice towards oneself demands an honest filtering through one's own reason and a critical observation of the entire avalanche of words that is propelled by the "propanganda machine." Justice obliges us to conduct ourselves always with good will and with love toward others; man created in the image of God is, by this fact, the supreme value after God. In the exercise of justice, love for man is above every other consideration and always plays the principal role.

Justice forbids the limiting of man's freedom by laws and decrees that become more and more numerous and convenient for the regime. It is worth recalling, to all of those who declare that they are acting in the name of humanism and the good of society, the words of a wise man: "The more the liberties of citizens are limited, the less human is the regime." It is justice and the right to truth that impel us to call for an end to the excesses of censorship, which gives a damning testimony of our times and presently keeps the public from knowing the truth.

In the name of justice, it is important to grasp and

stress the importance of the tremendous feeling of renewal that Solidarity is bringing to the mentality of Poland. It is no longer necessary to pass over in silence a small amount of immaturity, spontaneity, or perhaps even some excesses in Solidarity. This derives much more from a lack of experience than from bad faith. "This word," the Holy father said in speaking of *Solidarity* on June 2, 1982, "testifies to the great effort made by the workers in my country to maintain their true dignity."

It is unjust to attempt to form public opinion that accepts Solidarity's sole objective to have been the strikes that led to the current crisis in our country. In his letter of December 6, 1982, addressed to Parliament, the primate of Poland wrote, "It is important to state that for some time now the workers' unions and, in particular, the most powerful of them, Solidarity, have been struggling against the ploys of wildcat strikes."

And Bishop Majdanski, addressing the workers, stated, "It would be worth looking to other countries in which there is great abundance if strikes break out there over the decades. The reason for the crisis has its origin elsewhere."

Justice must grant each person his legitimate rights and therefore the right to work according to one's training. Justice likewise demands that dismissing people from their jobs for political reasons be absolutely forbidden. The primate of Poland spoke of this, January 2, 1982, in the following terms: "A very serious problem presently concerns the Church. It is the problem of dismissing from their jobs those who do not wish to quit the Solidarity union. We rise up against this injustice and this offense to the rights of man." In this manner the primate responded to the law unjustly promulgated under the direct order of the prime minister by General M. Janiszewski on December 17, 1981. Up to the present time, this problem has not been resolved.

Justice demands that workers be able to organize into unions as they see fit. In the encyclical *Laborem Exercens*, the Holy Father, John Paul II, stated:

> Professional organizations—unions must not be subordinated to the decisions of political parties nor should they any longer have direct links to them. Otherwise, they risk losing their main reason for existence, namely, the defense of the legitimate rights of workers in the area of the well-being of the whole of society, and they then become an instrument serving other ends.

Workers can judge for themselves how this problem is being tackled in our own country.

In the name of justice, youth must have the right to organize into associations reflecting its hopes and its ideals. Justice demands respect for the will of the majority in the election of rectors of academies; it demands that the choice made by students and university professors be respected and that scholarly and qualified people not be "stone-walled," sidetracked, or "left on the shelf" for the sole reason that they had the courage to express their opinions openly and come to the defense of students.

Justice gives us the right to preach from here, where for a year and a half the fervent prayer of suffering hearts has risen in behalf of the right and duty to appeal once more for the release of all political prisoners and compensation for injuries caused to them, particularly those injuries in the moral realm. We also have the right to appeal unconditionally for the freedom of those who have been placed under arrest for thirty-one months without trial or verdict. Agents of the judiciary must recall that, by the light of divine justice, man is more important than the letter of the law and that, in our country, laws and decrees are often utilized not only to search once again for truth but also to cause man to suffer. This profession dishonors itself in firing people who follow their conscience and not merely orders.

I am conscious of having mentioned merely a small number of social-justice problems. Each of you present here could speak at greater length, but let us limit ourselves today to what I have just mentioned.

I beg you to reflect—let us measure the courage that each of us expends in appealing for justice. To what extent is each one of us a promoter of justice by starting with himself, his family, and his circle of friends? It is frequently our moral passivity that is at the basis of injustice.

It is only by recalling the words of Jesus Christ—our justice must be greater than that of the scribes and the Pharisees—that we can accept the words of the Beatitudes: "Blessed are those who hunger and thirst for justice, for they shall be satisfied" (Matthew 5:6).

Amen.

JULY 1984

Homily (by Monsignor Bogucki)

Forty years have gone by in postwar Poland. Its political and social forces have changed. Even the frontiers of the country have changed in their size and dimensions. The very name of Poland has changed.

It is not my task to detail the successes and the failures of successive five-year plans in the economic and political realm. History records all of that. It remembers the great sufferings and humiliations of the nation. There can be no discussion about the fact that the Church has had an enormous influence on the spiritual formation of the nation during this difficult period in its history.

Thanks to bishops and to priests, the Church kept the people near God, comforted them, and enkindled hope. It was also for this purpose that we inaugurated the holy mass for the fatherland on the last Sunday of each month, in order to pray with all of the people for the prosperity of the fatherland and for God's protection of the nation. The mass is not closed to anyone. Quite the contrary, there are many who have found their way back to the Lord; there are many who understand their rightful place in the nation. These masses have calmed troubled spirits and relieved tensions.

We are following the example of the Holy Father, who prays ceaselessly for the fatherland and who, each Wednesday, publicly invokes our Lady of Jasna Gora to watch over the Polish nation. It is for this reason that we cannot give up this mass for the fatherland, and no one, if he cherishes the good of the church and the fatherland in his heart, can forbid it to us.

All of us, priests and faithful, respect the public and legal sector, which is the very basis of the social order. No priest among us is doing anything to the detriment of the fatherland. We do not betray it; we do not sell it out; we do not demoralize it. For every priest, insofar as he is "another Christ," is intended to offer mass, to proclaim the word of God, and—in accordance with the words of St. Paul—"Insist, refute and threaten, in season and out of season," to point out defects. A priest therefore cannot renounce this mission, which is given to him by Christ. It is meant to be exercised in accordance with his vocation and his conscience.

The prophets of the Old Testament play an important role in the nation. They watched over the purity of faith in the One God, correcting those who strayed, even reprimanding kings when they turned away from God. But they also knew how to console and comfort. This prophet role has been played out among the people of God by priests. Bishop Szczepanowski underwent martyrdom in the church at Skalka for having defended the moral order. In the Cathedral of Warsaw, Father Peter Skarga did not hesitate to raise his voice before the king and the nobility in order to denounce very courageously the excesses and the vices of the lords of that time who were leading the nation straight to Hell. Archbishop Szczesny Felinski was exiled for twenty years for having taken part openly in the January uprising against the czar. But *he* defended his honor as a priest and as a Pole. In return for having been able to speak the truth courageously and to defend the rights of the nation, Cardinal Stefan Wyszynski was arrested in a rather brutal fashion, practically at the throne of the Church of St. Anne—he describes it in his *Prison Notes*—and he was imprisoned for three years. But he did not bend.

Christ, the high priest, is the model of all priests. He did not seek to be a diplomat but he dared to criticize the Pharisees, the leaders of the nation, reproaching them for their hypocrisy and their lies; he called them "whitened sepulchers.''

Just as no one can prevent the sun from shining, no one can prevent a priest from proclaiming the truth. To proclaim the Word of God is not to enter the realm of politics, although the Church does have the right to intervene in the political arena each time that it acts against divine and human laws. It has the right to demand respect and social justice for man, to teach love of the fatherland, and to lift its voice in defense of the oppressed. It is precisely this service that is being fulfilled by priests. To attack priests is to attack the church; it is to attack the nation of which they are the light. ''You are the light of the world,'' Christ said to the Apostles. Priests act *for* the people and suffer *with* them.

The fatherland has always demanded sacrifice. Some soldiers accomplish this at barricades and in trenches. And priests, with their stoles and crosses in hand, fought alongside them at all fronts in order to defend the capital from invasion—some carrying a rifle, others a stretcher, others still a crucifix—such as Father Ignacy Slorupka, who fell with the cross in his hands on the fields of Ossowo as he was encouraging scouts into battle. We are celebrating the fortieth anniversary of the Warsaw Uprising. Priests marched alongside youth. Priests never abandoned the people, they were to be found in concentration camps; they suffered together and died under torture—priests such as St. Maximilian Kolbe who, to the question asked him as he stood before the rows of those being deported to Auschwitz: ''Who are you?'' responded, ''A Catholic priest.''

It is for this reason that the Polish Nation loves and respects its priests. One of our poets expressed it in these words: ''I have infinite respect for the servants of God who are the salt and the dew of the Polish earth.'' God has honored the Polish clergy by calling our great fellow countryman, John Paul II, to the Sea of Peter.

My dear friends, I had the intention of speaking to you today of something else, but the Holy Spirit breathes where he wills and he directed my thoughts in other ways, towards that which fills my heart and disturbs me. Considering the false accusations and unjust condemnations, I esteem it my duty to present to you, in the light of his own thoughts, the transparent personality of Father Jerzy Popieluszko, whom I consider one of our finest priests, zealous and full of the spirit of God, and one of the best Poles, generous and devoted with all his heart to the fatherland. All can attest that he incites no one to hatred or to vengance. Quite the opposite, he preaches love and forgiveness. He is not an agitator, but he does calm hearts which are in revolt! Of course it is possible to make a criminal out of every person, to demonstrate his faults by every means possible, without taking account of conscience and public opinion.

Father Jerzy is not an anarchist. he calls all of us to peace, to reason, to patience. The proof of this is the calm and the extraordinary seriousness that obtain during his services. He calms the effervescent spirits and he lowers tensions. I know that all of you here present, and not just yourselves, defend Father Jerzy by your fervent prayer.

We place our confidence in God that no one in Poland will ever do any evil to him.

The announced amnesty is a proof of clemency for those who have committed a misdemeanor, not for those who are innocent and who—by their words and by their actions—desire to do good for the fatherland. The benefits of this amnesty will be revealed at the moment when unconditional freedom is coupled with complete enjoyment of civil rights, freedom for the written and spoken word. For as the bishops wrote, the media cannot serve as the sole vehicle for spreading preferred ideology once the rights of the Solidarity union are restored. The hopes of the Holy Father expressed at Belvedere Palace will then be realized.

"Restoration," the Holy Father stated, "is indispensable for maintaining the reputation of Poland throughout the world." The Holy father repeated these words on July 25, last Wednesday, in St. Peter's Square.

At the end of forty years, society is worn out; it wants calm and a genuine working agreement in the spirit of mutual trust between society and the authorities so that by a common effort, as the Holy Father stated, there then can be built a better future for the Fatherland with the best interests of the nation and of the state guaranteed.

Up until now, there have been some extremely eloquent words contradicted by the facts, thereby creating a wider and wider gulf between the governed and the governing. That is why, in his appeal at Jasna Gora, the Holy Father declared "The state is first and foremost powerful by virtue of its concern for society, which is so clearly seen when the historical road taken by the nation is fully understood."

We want nothing else, my dear friends, than the fulfillment of the words of the Holy Father, namely, the total understanding of the historical road of the nation. We need not turn away from this one thousand-year history or direct the nation by force to the road of a foreign ideology.

It is this Polish national route that priests and all those who feel themselves responsible for the destiny of the nation are preserving. We must not haul them before tribunals for that or condemn them for it. The nation is patiently enduring humiliations, and it is bearing its cross while still remaining confident in the one who protects the Polish nation.

It is to you, therefore, that we address ourselves, speaking to you with the words of the Holy Father: "Mother, we have need of you now more than ever; take

into your maternal hands the heart and the mind of
Poland; take into your hands the destiny of our nation.''
    Amen.

AUGUST 1984

Homily

Throughout the course of our Nation's history, Mary, Mother of the Son of God, has been an inseparable element of its past. She chose Jasna Gora for the seat of her reign, and she did so in order that Poles might always feel themselves free—notably at the time of the nation's cruelest slaveries.

At Grunwald in 1410 as in Vienna in 1683, in 1920, during World War II, and since then, she has been the one who reinforces the hope of the Polish nation.

At the time of partition, especially in the Russian territory, a religious and Marian tone dominated patriotic demonstrations. The czarists also reacted against Marian hymns, which were preserved in the churches. The Cossack hordes saw their enemy in our Lady of Czestochowa. They searched homes looking for images with her likeness. They snatched up these images that were hanging like wordless tracts on the walls and the doors of houses. Functionaries of the czar and commissions of inquiry listened with a certain amount of fright to what were called "the deeds of war of the Lady of Jasna Gora," she whom they did not hesitate to designate a "major revolutionary" during the January insurrection.

Then in 1920, a short time after the return of independence, the bishops of Poland recrowned our Lady of Czestochowa as Queen of Poland. And in the solemn words of this action they declared, "Here, at Jasna Gora, in which each stone proclaims the miracles of your long-lived protection of our nation, we lift up our hands toward you, Mother of mercy, begging you to come to our aid at the moment when the country is in need." Mary had always been, for the nation, a Mother sustaining her children in faith and in the hope of one day seeing the situation of the martyred fatherland change.

She is to be found whenever the faith and hope poured into the image of the Black Madonna is awakened. Lechon has written: "She is seen in each peasant Polish home, at the church and in the shops, in a beautifully cast statue in the hands of someone who is in agony, and above the cribs of children."

In August 1980, through her likeness, she touched the dockyards of Gdansk and Szczecin, the mines of Silesia, and the steel mills of Warsaw. She even accompanied the outburst of patriotism in our Nation. She assisted at the birth of Solidarity.

Today, on this fourth anniversary of that birth, we have the right to remind ourselves in greater detail of the atmosphere of those warm days of August, days of uncertainty for our native land, colorful days, days of torment, of physical and spiritual fatigue; days during which, kneeling before improvised altars, with patriotic and religious songs on their lips, and with assistance from artists and intellectuals, the workers launched a vigorous appeal in behalf of the dignity of man and of work. Thus it was that the Polish nation's Solidarity was born.

Solidarity already had its roots in preceding appeals for truth and justice in 1956, 1968, 1970, and 1976. It had watered its roots with tears, pain, and the blood of workers; it watered them with the humiliation of the university youth. That is why it grew rapidly into a powerful tree that now, with its huge branches, covers the entire nation; and even though its growth was stormy, no one during the fifteen months of its legal activity was killed because of it. Solidarity, born in August 1980, is not the only union to be formed, but it is the inspiration of the entire nation for truth, justice, and liberty. The clear evidence that martial law had been launched against the entire nation, and not only against the union, confirms the fact that

Solidarity was national. It was a solidarity of the entire nation.

Two years ago in August, I said that Solidarity had been wounded and that blood continued to flow from the wound. But this wound was not deadly, for it is not possible to kill hope. Today we feel much better and have great admiration for our brothers who remained faithful to their ideals but now are out of prison. We feel much better, perceiving that the hope of 1980 is still alive and productive. This hope is more obvious today because it runs deeper in human hearts and minds. What is within the heart, what is deeply anchored in man, will not permit itself to cave in when faced with decrees and ordinances. I think that it would not be out of place here to recount a story that was told throughout a starving nation in Africa; its President had forbidden his subordinates to use the word *hunger*, threatening them with very severe penalties; he then announced to the entire world that the problem of hunger no longer existed in his country. In our country the problem exists and will continue to exist because Solidarity is the hope for possibly assuaging the hunger in the heart of man, the hunger for love, justice, and truth.

It is not permitted to misuse this word and to reserve it for a presumably less glorious past. This word is pronounced with respect by the entire world. The Holy Father stated that it was a "glorious word," and it has been awarded the loftiest award on earth, the Nobel Peace Prize.

The hopes of the month of August 1980 are still alive, and we have the moral duty of reaffirming them courageously in ourselves and in our brothers. We must get rid of fear that paralyzes and alienates the mind and heart of man. In this instance, I am repeating the sentence previously spoken in this place: that it is fitting only to have fear about betraying Christ for a few *denarii* of fleeting peace and quiet. We have the duty of witnessing to the truth of August 1980 in the same way that all the directors of the Solidarity union have witnessed for almost three years running.

We have the duty of demanding that the hopes of the nation be finally realized. It is very appropriate to do so with courage and balance. We need to take into account our own geopolitical situation but, at the same time, the situation must not be a convenient excuse for renouncing the rights due to our nation.

Finally, we need to sit around the table and seek a solution to all of our problems in a process of sincere dialogue that takes into account the welfare of the Fatherland. Instead of creating the fiction of pseudoconversations with organizations created out of nothing, we need to sit around a table with the credible representatives of the nation, with those in whom the nation has confidence, those on whom it has never turned its back. The bishops at one time wrote that the parties involved in the social agreement should be public authorities and credible representatives of social groups such as Solidarity, which enjoys such widespread recognition in society. We need to eliminate completely the barriers that prevent dialogue between the nation and the authorities. Dialogue should be conducted, above all, in an honest fashion—up to the point where amnesty will be obtained for all prisoners and those accused of political activities. It is important to compensate for the wrongs, especially the moral wrongs, committed against those who, in their own way, loved the Fatherland in a totally disinterested fashion. We need to guarantee all those who are in hiding the return to a normal life. They have already offered the great sacrifice of their activity on the altar of the fatherland.

The Polish nation has no hatred and is capable of a great deal of forgiveness, but this will only be at the price of a return to truth. For truth, and truth alone, is the primary condition for confidence. The nation, so sorely tried, will no longer show faith in hollow declarations.

Let us invoke the most Blessed Virgin, our Lady of Jasna Gora, on the day of Her feast, that she may help all of us in our fatherland to understand that it is not possible to build a house with lies, restrictions, and hatred. Let us invoke the most Blessed Virgin, our Lady of Jasna Gora, on the day of Her feast, that she may help all of us in our fatherland to understand that it is not possible to build a house with lies, restrictions, and hatred.

Let us use the words of the Holy Father, who prayed on August 4, 1983, as follows: "Mother! Perhaps it is important today more than ever that you take between your maternal hands the hearts and the minds of Poles, that you take between your hands the destiny of my nation."

May our blessing be addressed "to tired factory workers, to farmers in their fields, to educators and teachers in their weighty task of instruction, to scientists in their painstaking research, to health services concerned with our life and our health, and to all those who are building up the common good of our fatherland."

And let us pray, finally, with the words of a contemporary woman poetess:

Queen of Poland . . .
Your faithful people place themselves at Your feet
And beg you:
Give peace in our days
And Solidarity in our Hearts.
Amen.

SEPTEMBER 1984

Homily
   The biblical readings for this Sunday invite us to reflect on the commandment to love our neighbor and to discover that love forbids us to be indifferent when faced with the trials of another. The problem undoubtedly affecting love of neighbor, and a timely problem today in this beginning of September, in this beginning of the school year, is that of the school, of the Christian education of children and young people.
   In the Polish nation, Christian education has been bound up with the history of the fatherland, and it has had an influence in practically every sector of its life. We are not permitted to cut from present-day education everything that has been Polish for a thousand years. No one has the right to plow it up or to deform it, because the Christian system of education, based on Christ and upon his Gospel, has undergone serious trials during these most difficult days in the fatherland.
   The years following World War II were merely a whole series of struggles for the monopoly of atheistic education, for education without God, for casting God out of the hearts of children and young people. Polish Catholic society knows, at least in part, the wrongs and the moral damage with which it had to put up and with which it still has to cope as a result of the imposition of a program of atheistic religion upon believers. Moreover we feel the results of this in a very practical fashion each day. In its work, the school as an educational institution must depend on parents, since children belong to parents. It is not the state but mothers who bring children into the world. For this reason the school must not destroy in the souls of children the values that the family teaches.

The late lamented primate pointed this out very sternly: "The school is national and it belongs to the nation, to the family, to society, and not to a sect, a party, or a group whose vision, goals, and objectives are less glorious and sometimes even hostile and counterproductive to the nation and to the state, such as is the case in efforts to extinguish faith in the hearts of young people and children." In spite of the fact that it has been totally taken over by the state, the school must serve the family and the nation. It must bring to children and young people love for the Fatherland and an appreciation of national culture and our more than one-thousand-year-old history. It must not do so by stressing in every way possible that only the last forty years have been of benefit to the nation. Actually the Nation has not yet arrived at the point of discovering these benefits.

The school must take into consideration the nation, its needs, culture, and religion. When the state is not committed to such a school a much heavier responsibility falls upon parents, teachers, youth, and children.

The teacher must above all be a friend to the pupil. He must be a person who speaks the truth, a sincere teacher who does not serve the regime but who by virtue of his talent and his own authority, serves young people and children. Teachers must ever have in mind the fact that they are bringing up the young generation for the fatherland. They are watering their roots with an ancient and glorious past and not just for one or another fleeting regime without a future. Teachers cannot be conscious only of what is useful "for today" but rather of what is needed to serve future generations. I am not speaking to you today of the religious education of children and young people by catechism or of the importance of catechism for all Christians. This would appear to be so self-evident that it is not necessary to explain it to anyone who views education from the aspect of the whole child.

The second problem that flows from love of neighbor with respect to the good he does and the evil he commits, and which we have the obligation to challenge, is what took place last week. I will now be accused of entering into politics; but in a country in which politics tries with impunity, to invade every sector of social life, it is all the more important to approach certain problems from their moral aspect.

This problem is very disturbing; it pertains to the recent statement of the government spokesman during his press conference: "Certain experts in penal law propose to introduce into the penal code a number of new penalties: by simple decree a person who acts against the state or has been shown to be disrespectful of the constitutional principles of the system will be automatically deprived of his civil rights and banished from Poland for a determined period of time. The experts who are going to argue for this position indicate that exile is not a judicial procedure unknown to systems of jurisprudence in the capitalistic world" (*Zycie Warszawy*, September 5, 1984, p. 2).

Let us lay aside the fact that by such a judicial measure the authorities of Poland are rolling back history to the beginning of the Middle Ages; let us lay aside the question: since when has the capitalistic model of jurisprudence become a paradigm for a country endowed with a "progressive and humanitarian" system? But the very germination of such an idea within the minds of certain Poles is a *crime* against the nation. The government spokesperson does not have in mind ordinary offenders of the common law but the best sons of the fatherland, who are courageously opposing the destruction of the very soul of the nation. The spokesperson finally declared, and I quote, "Certain countries situated on continents other than Europe are ready to welcome, under certain conditions, persons who would eventually be expelled from Poland" (ibid., *Zycie Warszay*).

It would perhaps be useful for people professing such ideas to begin by first of all verifying their own links to the fatherland and their own level of patriotism. And . . . perhaps the nation would have nothing against their going into exile, not necessarily outside of Europe? During the state of war, the Holy Father referred to this idea: "It is not necessary that Poland lack a place for Poles! Every man has the right to his fatherland; no one can be condemned to emigration." No one, therefore, has the right to deprive anyone of his fatherland in which he has dwelt for generations. In our prayers let us present these two very difficult and equally important problems to reflect upon them during the coming week.